OVERCOMING DADDY ISSUES- SORROW TO VICTORY

Stories of Healing from Father Wounds

CHERYL BURTON

Contents

Acknowledgments

This book is for the woman or girl who wants to release her father hunger and stop being controlled by it and instead develop into a healthy, productive person who fulfills her dreams.

Daddy Issues would not have developed or been relevant unless the women I interviewed were willing to tell their story. I appreciate their transparency and readiness to showcase their pain to foster growth of other women. I relish my journey of grief that nagged me until I agreed to share my experience with the hope to benefit women with a similar challenge.

I value Robert S. McGee's' paperback *Father Hunger*. His book opened my eyes to my hurt and disappointment with my dad. I agree with McGee that a woman has a hollow place in her heart that longs for the blessing that only a father can give.

I thank my Lord and Savior Jesus Christ who has protected me during all my years of foolish behaviors even though I didn't acknowledge or know Him. In hindsight I see His protective hand.

Surprisingly, I am grateful for my involvement with the narcissists, cheaters and liars. These men taught me who I didn't want in my life and how to avoid their destructive behaviors.

Introduction

The jury is no longer out on whether a father provides value to a daughter. There is plenty of credible evidence that indicates he does. Even the renowned psychologist Sigmund Freud said, "I cannot think of any need in childhood as strong as the need for a father's protection." Yes, single women raise daughters who are competent and reliable. This book isn't for them. My purpose is to discuss the girls who experienced and overcame significant daddy issues. Each story exhibits the daughter's perspective of her father's damaging impact and what each did to achieve success despite her obstacles.

It is challenging for a woman to be a single parent regardless of ethnicity. However, African American women have an extreme burden to bear. The number of black men in prison reduces their pool of available mates. According to the Census Bureau (2013) forty-nine percent of black men ages 18-34 are institutionalized; in the ages thirty-five to sixty- four forty-seven percent are imprisoned. The National Association for the Advancement of Colored People (NAACP) 2019 Criminal Justice fact sheet reports that black people are incarcerated at more than five times the rate of whites.

What are the human costs? Without a daddy, girls grow up without a father's support and influence. They may seek love and affirmation from other men increasing sexually transmitted diseases and teenage pregnancy. Meager income forces the children to live in impoverished conditions and attend poorly performing schools. Life in dilapidated housing can exacerbate Asthma development. The sons of prisoners are likely to act out aggressively, use or sell drugs and join their parent in prison. One lawyer reported that he saw the grandfather, father and son in the same prison.

Incarceration takes a toll on the men too. After release the men receiving a callback or job offer is reduced by an estimated fifty percent. When I counseled ex-offenders, I was astonished to learn of their catch 22. Even service jobs like McDonalds' wouldn't hire them until they had been out for five years. They had a two-week window to become employed before the parole officer sent them back to prison. The only available jobs were day laborers, roofing or construction. Some states have since made changes that enable employment at an extensive variety of businesses.

Infectious diseases are rampant in the congested prison system. One report said fifteen percent of jail inmates and twenty-two percent of prisoners reported having Tuberculosis, Hepatitis B and C, HIV/AIDS or sexually transmitted diseases (STD's). Lateshia Beachum, Washington Post writes that" in the United States researchers estimate that 1.3 percent of prisoners have HIV and 16.4 percent of prisoners have hepatitis C." In the medical journal the Lancet the researchers concluded "that the spread of the disease is low during incarceration. However, it is difficult to continue treatment once prisoners are released. A researcher, Chris Breyer said the lack of resources is often the reason for a person becoming more infectious." Not only will the person have difficulty securing employment he may expose others to his disease.

An additional source of personal sadness results from my limited knowledge of the reasons women settle for a baby daddy. According to the Urban dictionary he is the biological father who can't buy his child diapers, formula or clothes. He may have access to the woman for sex or her wallet, but doesn't marry her. Some women have more than one baby daddy. It is naive to assume that dire social ills are correctable by a book. But it is a start, recognition of a problem can be an impetus to developing a solution.

Male bashing is not my goal. There are wonderful, involved fathers who sacrifice and contribute to raising daughters as a single parent or in a dual-parent home. My targets are the men who parented poorly or not at all. I will expose the dark side of the way father wounds can distress a daughter. I want to empower women to make wise choices when considering a mate because of the impact the decision has on future generations. The National Centering on Fathering reports that 71% of teenage pregnancies are from fatherless homes. The Fatherless Generation writes that "85% of all youths in prison come from fatherless homes according to Fulton County, Georgia and Texas Department of Correction,1992."

I am grateful to the black and white, women and girls who told their stories, occasionally in graphic detail. They are females who live in the United States and range in age from 14-73 years old. Pseudonyms' provide them anonymity. Their interview occurred in person or by phone. The recounted story incorporates the speakers dialogue. My minor alterations improved the flow of the text.

The book is divided into two parts. Part one reports fifteen experiences ranging from the weak father to the disappointment dad. Unfortunately, I was unable to provide a story of the impact of a fathers' death on his daughter. I hope the success of the contributors will spur you forward to achieve healing of your own.

If you want personal coaching to assist you in your therapeutic journey contact me at https://www.cheryleads.com/. Doing deep work with a coach who will challenge you is an effective way to achieve greater insight. I will provide an environment of no judgment or criticism.

At the end of most stories are questions designed to advance self-awareness. The challenge is in not deceiving yourself with an inauthentic answer. Before writing the response, ask yourself these questions; what is the truth and am I recording my self-affirming version of the truth? Know that dredging up memories of past hurts may be difficult but once truth is exposed healing can begin.

Ignore the temptation to scan the questions and not answer them. If you do you may be avoiding a vital way to improve your self-understanding.

The interview questions, titled Codependency questions are at the end of part one. I've included a list to determine if a woman is 'thirsty,' (excessively needy).

Part two contains a discussion of men who are poor candidates for marriage. I've included the most glaring ones; the narcissist, the sociopath, the commitment-phobe, the psychopath and the misogynist. I've also listed the red flags that signal danger.

Please provide your candid review on Amazon. Your feedback tells me if I achieved the goal of the book.

To learn self-leadership strategies that will improve your ability to influence yourself and others visit my Blog at
https://www.cheryleads.com/

Follow me on Facebook at
https://www.facebook.com/maximizeselfcb

Connect with me on LinkedIn.
https://www.linkedin.com/in/caburtoncoach/

Foreword

I have thought about the impact of a father on his daughter for several years. When I watched programs or read stories about women making poor life decisions with men, I rightly guessed, it was because they hadn't experienced the guidance of a loving dad. I often discussed my thoughts about the power of a father-daughter relationship with my life-long friend Brenda Branch. Although, she couldn't personally relate to my angst, she patiently listened. Because Brenda has known me since I was thirteen and she was fourteen and we have experienced marriage, parenting, parental death, divorce, educational pursuits, and professional connections, I asked her to tell the reader the reasons she believes I am qualified to write about daddy issues.

Brenda said," I have known Cheryl for fifty-nine years since high school. We worked together for seven years as respiratory therapists. We socialized during our single years and as married couples. I flew to Los Angeles, California and we traveled back to St. Louis, MO. in her Volkswagen Beetle convertible. During the trip we shared fun and secrets like women do. Cheryl possesses the ability to ask meaningful questions; she challenges me to provide a well-thought-out answer. She has a keen interest in other people's opinions and the driving forces behind their decisions. Cheryl is concerned about what matters to the individual. She is a reliable person. I witnessed the many disheartening challenges in Cheryl's personal life. Cheryl studied and researched to find answers to her compelling questions as I have known her to do. She commits to educating herself to gain deeper understanding in her areas of interest. This book is the culmination of her experiences, reality, occasional frustrations but most of all her heart. Cheryl realized that if she had questions, she wasn't alone in her thoughts. This book is a straight forward, easy read that will enlighten and give you the courage to face your struggles and release any emotional baggage."

A dad holds the key to his daughter's heart.

Part One:
Father Stories

Wounds from daddy issues penetrate the soul and are tough to heal.

I have met people whom I have said have 'issues; And indeed, girls and women without the guidance and direction of an involved father experience problems or concerns.

Chapter 1
The Weak Father: Kiara's Story

What kind of father mistreats a daughter during her formative years and then expects to be cared for when he is old? The weak father. The characteristics of a weak father include suffering from addiction, chronic unemployment, guilt-tripping the daughter into providing favors for him and being dependent on his daughter for survival. Reference Catherine Huang, YouTube; Psych.2 GO.net. Catherine labels this father as ruined. I call him weak.

A weak father doesn't have the internal fortitude or character to provide a strong groundwork for a daughter. These flaws could have resulted from poor parenting he experienced, his drug or alcohol use or, peer influence.

Kiara was an infant during her father's abuse. Her maternal grandmother told her the story. The grandmother saw the father carrying the infant Kiara upside down through an alley. She chased him and demanded he give her the baby. Kiara was wearing a tee-shirt and a urine-soaked diaper. Kiara's dad chose drug use over employment. The 19-year-old mother worked and left Kiara with her dad. The grandmother took over Kiara's care after the incident. When Kiara heard about her father's treatment of her as an infant it initiated her belief the world wasn't safe.

Kiara said," I don't remember living with my dad; he was in prison because he stabbed a 'dude.' "The dad told her, "I'm not responsible for his death. I stabbed him; he died." Not accepting responsibility is common in the weak individual.

"When I was a child, there were a few phone calls and letters between my dad and me. I missed having a dad. Aged ten or eleven,

I started writing to him. That stopped because my grandmother and mother read the letters before, I sent them. I found out because they told me I couldn't ask my dad why he killed someone. I had sealed the message and they violated my privacy. Granny and mom said, 'you're too young to know his reason.' I stopped writing to dad after that. I felt hurt and betrayed. I never bonded with my dad. At thirty-nine, I'm still getting to know him. Our relationship has been on and off. I don't know what it's like to have a caring father." When asked to describe the relationship, she'd like, she listed honesty, openness, ability to talk with each other, lack of judgment, and the capability to discuss emotions.

"My father is an addict with the same mindset and mentality of an addicted person. He is a narcissistic little boy." According to Roger P. Watts, Ph.D.; How the Addicted Brain Hijacks the Mind, Mental Help.net, "addiction is a brain disease, not a mind disease. Addiction affects the physical organ we call the brain. The after-effects of brain disease result in a loss of willpower, the inability to make good choices, defensiveness, and denial."

Kiara's father lived with her and her husband after release from prison. Two dysfunctional men in one house created disaster. One day an argument ensued, and the father sliced the husband's hand. After being kicked out, the father pleaded with Kiara to let him return. When she refused, he accused her of choosing her husband over him. The fragile father/ daughter relationship splintered.

Kira said, "my ideal father would be loving, protective, giving, open, trustworthy, and financially stable. None of these qualities exist in my biological father."

I asked Kiara to describe the characteristics of her husband; she said, "he is loving, not open, giving, not financially stable, an alcoholic, and narcissistic. I married my dad." Kiara selected a husband who treated her like her father and stepfather did. She married the familiar behaviors of alcoholism, verbal, and physical abuse. I asked her if she used her husband to try to rescue her dad? She said, "yes."

"I am attracted to men in jail or on their way to jail. Each one has been several years older than me. I believe I'm looking for my father. I say I want a healthy interaction but my behaviors are self-destructive."

When a woman doesn't believe in her value the entry requirements for an involvement with her are low. Throw her a few bread crumbs and a hungry woman will eat whether the food is tasty or spoiled.

Kiara is suspicious of men who are too kind." I think they can't be trusted because they're hiding something, or maybe I don't think I'm good enough for them." Does her not feeling worthy of love explain her selection of broken, unhealthy men, that she could attempt to 'fix' or be superior to? Does low self-worth fuel Kiara's rejection of healthy and too nice men?

During Kiara's childhood her mother remarried and had two daughters. Instead of gaining allies, she experienced their bullying and ridicule about her appearance and being a prisoners' daughter. Her stepfather was emotionally abusive and continuously criticized her deep chocolate color and apple-shaped body." "Why don't you lose weight?" he yelled. "Food was the only comfort I had. I wanted a father who hugged me when I was upset and told me I was pretty."

Kiara is a poster child for Fatherless-Daughter Syndrome. A syndrome is a group of symptoms. This syndrome includes an ongoing battle with self-esteem, a sense of value-lessness, and difficulty forming healthy, intimate associations. Kiara said," I don't remember when I haven't felt depressed."

Kiara is also codependent; she depends on the endorsement of another person for her self-worth and value. Some therapists have expanded or changed to another term for codependency. Two changes I'm aware of are Self-love Deficit Disorder (SLDD) Ross Rosenberg, M.ED., LCPC and Trauma Based Relating or PTSD-type feelings Kristi Pikiewicz, Ph.D. Codependency has transitioned from merely the relationship between a caregiver and an alcoholic or chemical addict to encompass self-destructive behaviors. Kiara's answers to questions on codependency reveal some of these conducts. Kiara tends to put others' needs before hers and overdoes or works too hard.

Kiara has poor boundaries, and says yes, 99.5% of the time, and ends up making promises to too many people. A hallmark of codependency is the tendency to put other people's needs before theirs. Codependents haven't learned to set healthy boundaries. Kiara says, "even though I overbook, I feel guilty because I should have been able to fit them in. Sometimes I feel shame and I don't feel good. I beat myself up for not helping. I enjoy being needed because it fulfills something in me when I take care of someone. I get depressed when I'm not providing nursing."

People who experience shame tend to believe there is something wrong with who they are not just what they do. As you read this book, you'll see several women admit to feeling shame. Although their reason varies the similarity is their belief that they are flawed. United with indignity is low self-esteem and the idea of being a damaged person.

Kiara says, "I know what my needs are and believe I deserve to have them fulfilled." But Kiara doesn't always act on her belief. She has been involved in unhealthy connections that are verbally, physically, and or emotionally abusive. Kiara acknowledges that communication, stability, and trust have been absent in her involvements with men. She has been either too passive or aggressive in personal associations. Although she has occasionally cared too much about others' opinions or judgments Kiara explains that, "It depends on whether it is a family member or a friend." She says she recognizes what others are doing wrong, but, "I try not to judge, but sometimes I end up judging."

Kiara admits she attempts to control people or situations. She says," I worry a lot; about my dogs, the weather, or people. I overeat, still using food for comfort."

Thankfully, Kiara has chosen to seek psychological health. She has received the care and guidance of a mental health professional. Her career path permits her to help others without enabling them. Kiara is a caregiver for Hospice or terminally ill patients, and she works as the House Manager for persons with a mental disability. The dual benefit is she feels more like a person of worth because she is servicing other's needs.

Kiara has the God-given spiritual gift of mercy. According to Dr. Larry Gilbert, Church Growth.org. the person with this gift "empathizes emotionally and experiences what the victim goes through." A disadvantage of this gift is Kiara's overattachment to her clients. When a patient dies, she admits," it feels like a part of me has died." Dr. Gilbert says," health workers and other caregivers are sometimes dragged down by taking other peoples' problems home with them." Kiara responded to the death of a favorite patient by lying on the floor and crying.

She satisfies her desire to be in control because she can implement the care of her clients as prescribed by their doctor. Her patients are usually glad to see her. She demonstrates extra care by buying toiletries for them with her money. The caregiver role fits Kiara perfectly because she thrives on being needed.

In some of her dating experiences, Kiara acted 'thirsty.' She admits, "I had to be in an involvement; I chose men who wouldn't give me space. My first boyfriend was twenty-four; I was sixteen. Yes, I've had obsessive thoughts about a man I liked. I have resorted to stalking a boyfriend; one example is a friend and I switched cars so I could track my cheating boyfriend without him recognizing my auto. I verbally assaulted another boyfriend while he was at work and with a customer; I thought he was cheating on me with the patron.

I'm embarrassed at flying off the handle, screaming and causing a commotion. I've been upset more than happy in most of my entanglements. Even when I discovered deceit I still stayed. I didn't want to feel like I lost what I had already invested. I endured a lot of stuff and bad behaviors from males. I have tolerated being lonely in relationships but I believe it is better to have somebody than nobody. Isn't it true that there's no gain without pain? I agree with the philosophy, 'it's better to have a piece of a man than no man at all. So, I'm going to take what I got and work with it.' Without a man I felt unbearably empty. I tolerated being punched, choked, slapped and downgraded with name-calling. I told myself I deserved it. I didn't leave an abusive relationship because dating is scary; at least I know what I'm dealing with in the abusive union. Yes, I believe it's true the devil you know is better than the devil you don't. Pain and mistreatment had been my norm. I learned to wake-up, cry, and go on."

"I tried to control the behaviors of my alcoholic husband. When he was angry, I kept him calm. I hid his liquor or poured salt in it so he wouldn't drink it. I took his picture to the convenience store where he walked to get alcohol and asked the clerk not to sell to him; my husband had to walk further if he wanted his drink."

"I am guilty of using different methods to self-soothe when I feel lonely. Food is my primary choice. I gained over one-hundred pounds. Sometimes I play video games, call friends, or drink until I can sleep."

Kiara may be good at nurturing others, but she has abandoned herself. She is a volunteer victim with a scarcity mindset who has made peace with her poor self-esteem. Persons with a scarcity mindset have usually experienced inadequate amounts of attention, affirmation, affection, and material possessions. She has given her power to the men in her life. Her actions tell them you can mistreat me, and I will stay, and I won't require love or support from you. Her behaviors shout I don't love myself and I don't expect you to care for me either.

Her self-sabotage began in childhood. She is a classic example of deprivation attachment. Her parent's inability to meet her needs left her feeling hollow and insignificant. Her sisters and peer group exacerbated the problem with bullying and discrimination. Because Kiara felt worthless, she only dealt with men who had as much or more psychological baggage than her. Plus, if the other person is worse Kiara can avoid looking at her faults.

Kiara can start her healing process by becoming comfortable being alone and content. If she can't stand being alone with herself how can she reasonably expect someone else to be alone with her? Kiara doesn't need someone to complete her. The problem will be fixed when Kiara repairs her fractures. It's an erroneous assumption that because happiness has been elusive, that means she'll never have it. It is never too late to become her best self. It begins with her banishing the idea that misery should be a companion; that is her volunteer victim talking. Kiara can also consider the downside of hooking her value to the opinion of another person.

Kiara's not alone in the desire to hear she's worthwhile from someone else. But the same words that praise can be used to control and manipulate. The more relevant terms are the ones Kiara says to herself.

Kiara has separated from her abusive, alcoholic husband and distanced herself from her weak father. Now, her challenge will be the' missing phase'. The most impactful stage of 'missing' is the beginning. The reasons for the separation fade and the good qualities and enjoyable activities enlarge. Kiara's test is not to be deceived and to stay focused on the purpose (s) for the goodbye.

Kiara has to silence the destructive chatter in her mind. Damaging self-talk enlarges self-loathing. She must stop trying to escape through sleeping or eating. Food can't fill an emptiness of the soul. Life is for living, not avoiding. Instead of overeating, she can confront what is eating her. Every day she can choose to become healthy and a person worthy of self-respect. If she needs help on her journey, she can invest in a coach; or talk with a friend who has her best interest at heart. She can set a weight loss and exercise goal that will develop the body she admires. She can practice gratitude for what she has every day; her physical and spiritual health, a fulfilling job, friends, pets she loves, and the ability for self-empowerment. When she becomes mentally and emotionally healthy, she will interest a stable companion. The Law of Attraction contends that we lure what we are and not what we want.

A summary of ways to overcome the influence of a weak father:

Accept that you won't be able to change him. He must be willing to do the tough work of self-examination and behavior change.

Maintain clearly defined boundaries for your interaction with him.

Stop hoping he will be an active parent and satisfy your own needs.

Develop a healthy plan for self-soothing that doesn't involve overeating or drug use.

Set aside time for daily reflection to improve self-awareness.

Engage in activities that improve your self-respect.

Create a template of the characteristics of your ideal partner.

Write in a journal to monitor your progress.

Don't maintain a close association with toxic people. Enhance your spiritual self.

Implement a growth plan with measurable tools for self-development. Read growth-enhancing books, attend classes, watch podcasts, or invest in residential or on-line training courses. Find a support, mastermind, or meet-up group to interact with people who help your improvement. Hire a coach or mentor to keep you accountable and to ensure you maintain desirable changes.

Seek advice from a friend who will tell you the truth rather than support your misconceptions.

Don't permit other people's labels to define you.

Learn to manage your problems and rescue yourself. Your self-esteem will soar.

Decide not to be a victim of your history. Victims manage their lives according to the orders of others.

Don't listen to unproductive self-talk.

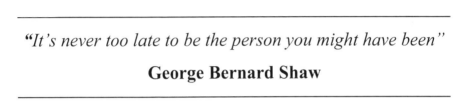

"It's never too late to be the person you might have been"

George Bernard Shaw

Your Action Plan

Reflection:

Spend a designated time each day in stillness. The process involves sitting comfortably in a quiet area free of disturbances. Close your eyes and relax your body. Take three-five slow deep breaths in and out through your nose, blowing out twice as long as you breathe in. Say a positive 'I am' statement, e.g., 'I am in control of my mind and my thoughts'; 'I am developing my best self'; 'I am honest with myself and others'. It is vital to use 'I am' statements you can believe.

A noisy mind with random thoughts is ordinary in the beginning; keep practicing until peacefulness predominates and the 'I am' ideas are preeminent. As you improve ask your subconscious to reveal the reason(s) for different behaviors and thoughts. Reflection calms your mind, clears unnecessary thoughts, and provides dynamic growth development.

Identify your top needs and how you plan to satisfy them.

_____

_____

_____

_____

_____

What healthy ways will you self-soothe?

_____

_____

_____

_____

_____

Identify the tools you'll use for self-improvement:

_____

_____

_____

_____

_____

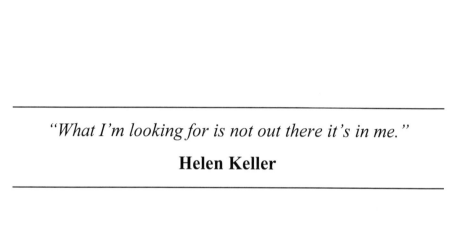

"What I'm looking for is not out there it's in me."

Helen Keller

Chapter 2
Absent Father: Dad I Never Knew You

"Who am I as a woman, and will I be valuable to a man?"

Cheryl Burton

Marietta is a lovely, petite woman with ash blonde hair and sky-blue eyes. Pain filled her eyes and tears wet her cheeks as she told of the impact of never meeting her father." Daddy was a rolling stone pausing long enough to impregnate my mother but not to meet me. My dad denied my mother and me; he never provided financial, emotional, or psychological support. I think he was immature and irresponsible. When I heard he died, I felt more alone than ever. His death erased a part of my life that will never be known. I still struggle to forgive him."

"When I learned my father had been married during the affair with my mom that reinforced my opinion of him. He was a cheater too." Does Marietta's dads' other commitment justify his un-involvement with Marietta? No. I believe he didn't know or care about the price his daughter would pay for his absence. Not only did Marietta not know her father but she was ignorant of his side of the family, her roots, and her genetic history. There is a cost for every action.

"Growing up, I never thought I was good enough, pretty enough, smart enough, feminine enough, or worthy of love. I was jealous of friends who had a father. I felt desperate for male attention. I wanted to be liked and accepted but I never thought I had enough to offer. I believed if my dad was disinterested in me, that means I'm not lovable. How can I expect other men to value me when my dad didn't?"

Children think concretely about self-worth. If daddy demonstrates he thinks his daughter is desirable beyond her sexuality, that is what she will believe. If he doesn't, she'll gravitate toward poor self-value.

"My mom never demonstrated any affection toward me. She never hugged or touched me." Marietta's mom mimicked the behavior of her dad. Marietta says, I didn't have a man in my life to hug, praise, or validate me."

"My mom and I lived with my aunt and uncle. My uncle was a hard worker with high expectations; I tried hard to live up to his standards. When my mom and I moved from that environment, I felt ripped from stability with a typical family to a house with a mentally ill uncle. When we were home alone, my uncle came into my bedroom, frightened, I was able to escape outside. I always felt depressed, nervous, and fearful; I didn't believe my mom would protect me. When I was about eight a childhood female friend molested me. I told my mother but, she said I had to continue to visit the girl because we rented an apartment from the girls' father. My family had a code of silence.

"As a teenager, I drank a lot and smoked pot to escape my pain. I tried cocaine once. I started dating at fourteen and met my future husband at fifteen. I performed oral sex on my dates as a way of getting them to like me. I desperately wanted their acceptance because I didn't get approval from my dad."

Marietta is similar to other women with absent dads; she ignored her wants and shifted focus to the male's desires. Marietta traded her body for temporary affection. Marietta said," I didn't have intercourse until I was seventeen. I decided it was time I wasn't a virgin anymore and I was curious about the sexual experience."

"My mom expected me to be a good girl and always be kind. I had to follow the rules; no smoking or cussing; act perfect. I never felt perfect."

Marietta confesses," as an adult, I still use alcohol to dull my pain and anesthetize the anguish."

"My husband was my hope for healing the father wound but he was dealing with his pain. I wanted him to fill my empty love tank but he hasn't. He grew up with a schizophrenic mother and an emotionally distant, perfectionist father. I blame myself for choosing a husband who doesn't fulfill my emotional and psychological needs."

"I expected my husband to serve as a surrogate father for many years. As my substitute dad, he managed our finances, made sure I went to work on time, maintained my car, and did most of our home repairs. I was frustrated by his unwillingness to hire someone to do maintenance but his perfectionistic ways ruled that out. I am learning to appreciate his desire to save the family money by being Mr. fix-it and doing simple car upkeeps. I've stopped complaining about the length of time it takes. I'm practicing gratitude for my family, my lovely home, and my ability to work. I am deepening my relationship with God. I'm learning to accept I will never have the father of my dreams. I also appreciate my husband actively participating in raising our sons. He served as their soccer coach and provided them a male's perspective about life. He has modeled morality and fidelity to his family."

Have you noticed the similarities between the daughter with a weak father and the daughter with an absent father? To summarize the results of having an absent father are:

Emotional suffering

Troubled behavior

Lingering depression

Poor self-esteem

Unstable foundation

Longing for male affection

Unhealthy efforts for male validation

Wearing a will, you love me banner?

Lack of self-confidence

Drug use to escape reality

The feeling of being tossed in a dumpster and deserted without suitable resources.

It is believing in unlovability, attached to the constant fear of rejection and abandonment by men.

Reluctance to get too close in relationships because of potential pain.

Marietta denies behaving as a thirsty woman. "I didn't pursue men; I wanted them to come to me. I was the cheater sometimes involved with three-four men at a time. I didn't try to control a man's conduct. If I liked him, I would feel severe loneliness when I wasn't with him."

In response to the co-dependency questions Marietta said, "I tend to put other's needs before mine because I enjoy being needed. I don't dwell on my wants. I responded yes when I should have said no, I don't have good boundaries. I've gotten into unhealthy entanglements when I wanted to prove I was worthy. I needed validation. I became what the other person required. I didn't stop until my forties. I still care too much about other people's opinions. I'm getting better but can use improvement. I don't feel like I have much control. I worry a lot, especially about my two sons. I'm concerned about my lack of power over what might happen to them in life. I feel more depressed than frustrated with other people. I am good at knowing what people are doing wrong in their life. At work I fulfill the requirements according to my energy level."

Remember, the hallmark of codependency is self-destructive activities accompanied by depression, low self-worth, and disordered relationships.

Despite Marietta's family difficulties she attended college and earned a license as a health care professional before marriage. She specializes in helping patients with lung disease improve their exercise tolerance. She is currently a clinical instructor for health care students at a major medical facility. Her two grown sons are pursuing their education. She has been married for over thirty years. Marietta struggled with forgiving her mom and dad for their frailties. "I think I have forgiven my mom, but I haven't thought about my father, so I guess I have to say no. When it comes to my father, forgiving him is something I need to do."

When I suggested she seeks counseling or coaching, Marietta said," I can't. It would hurt too much to open the scarred wounds." Pain induced injuries, even if covered by scar tissue, are unlikely to heal.

Marietta concludes, "the thing that helps me the most is accepting that God is my true Father, and He is superior to any earthly father I could have ever known."

My counsel for Marietta and women suffering from unforgiveness is to learn to forgive people who have wronged you. Holding on to resentment and unforgiveness can cause stress, depression, and delay spiritual growth. For the person who refuses to face her truth, she is likely to remain bound to negative emotions. Those emotions keep you stuck in the past. Their presence makes you a prisoner of events you can't change. According to Don Colbert, MD., Deadly Emotions. "The mind and body are linked; how you feel emotionally can impact the way you feel physically. An emotional roller coaster saps a person physically and psychologically, which can leave both mind and body depleted of energy and strength."

Two other aspects of father absence were said to be the pain of never having someone to call daddy, and the sorrow at not having a partner at the school-sponsored father-daughter dance.

How to Overcome Father Absence

Accept that your parents did what they knew to do at the time; your dad, according to his character and your mom, according to hers. Forgive yourself for the choices you made to bandage your hurts and search for significance.

If you're struggling with forgiveness, you're choosing to remain wounded by events you can't change. Accept that your father decided not to be a part of your life. It is not an indictment against you; the fault is his. Write a letter to your father telling him how his absence impacted you. Destroy the message along with your regrets for not having a relationship. Or position two chairs facing one another, imagine your father seated across from you-tell him how his absence affected you. Don't associate your value with your father's presence. Stop pitying yourself for what you didn't have; focus on what you did have. Don't engage in destructive self-talk. Identify the activities you enjoy and do them.

If learning about your father's relatives is imperative- to research for them, use one of these methods:

www.Ancestry.com

www.NAMUS.com (National Missing and Unidentified Persons System: they provide free DNA testing and reveal relatives)

Be aware that some people don't want a relationship with you.

If you struggle with shame, not feeling worthy based on who you are is not uncommon.

"Our greatest wounds integrated become strength."

Anne French

Your Action Plan

List self-care activities:

_____

_____

_____

_____

_____

What will you do to improve your self-esteem?

_____

_____

_____

_____

_____

List the words you say to yourself that make you feel worthless.

_____

_____

_____

_____

_____

Cheryl Burton

List the words or phrases that improve your self-worth. Substitute these words or phrases for the disempowering ones.

_____

_____

_____

_____

_____

Chapter 3
The Perfect Father - Searching for Mr. Right: Raven's Story

"A great dad captivates his daughter's heart."

Cheryl Burton

Why would a woman who describes her father as a perfect dad experience father hunger? Raven says, "I'm hungry because my desire for a husband like my dad hasn't been satisfied." I asked what made your dad perfect? Raven shared twelve characteristics; "daddy made me feel special like I was daddy's girl; he teased me in a fun way and was a fantastic jokester who created laughter in our home. Daddy was wise, gave great advice, and encouraged me to work for what I wanted. His peers, congregation, and family respected him as a genuine man of God. He pastored two churches and ministered to anyone with a spiritual or physical need. Daddy modeled the biblical principles he preached. He relied on the Lord to provide for his nine children. He knew how to manage when we didn't have meat, he hunted rabbits. He carved out time to cherish me and provide me lots of affection. He assured me he was my protector. He believed a man is not a man unless he can take care of his kids. I saw my dad rise above all his restrictions and live above the 'see' level. That means to look beyond your problem and see God and believe He will work it out. When a believer uses 'see,' the problem is turned around and changed. Daddy was a sharp dresser and well-groomed. My dad was my world."

Raven's eyes saddened as she said, "my dad was as near to perfect as a man can be." Raven is describing a unicorn man. In case you don't know, a unicorn man is attractive, monogamous, funny, employed, communicative, caring, and interested in the woman.

"One of my challenges is I don't feel pretty enough to attract this man. I'm not beautiful like my sister. She is striking-everyone said so. I feel ordinary in comparison. I also stuttered as a child. Kids made fun of me when I talked. I felt fearful all the time, especially when I had to read aloud. I had poor self-esteem during childhood and adolescence."

"As a child, I felt lonely for my mom. She had nine children and always wanted to sacrifice for everyone, but I didn't get much attention from her."

"I began dating at sixteen. I started having sex at eighteen with a man who said he loved me. Those words made me feel special. Experience has taught me that men become what I tell them I want. Although my goal is to be up-front about my desires, some men have used that information to deceive me about who they are. Later they change from Dr. Jekyll (good) to Mr. Hyde (evil)."

"My first son was born when I was twenty-two. He died at eighteen months of lung disease. It was painful to watch him need the help of a machine to breathe. After being taken off the ventilator his heart stopped twice (cardiac arrest). After the second full arrest in which his heart and breathing stopped God took him home. His death was responsible for me choosing a career in health care."

Raven said, "My dad died two years ago. When I think about him, I feel happy, sad, and lonely. I have a deficit-a lonely place that only his presence could fill."

"Yes, I have an excessive need to feel valued. I feel hurt if I'm not. I want people to appreciate me so I have to be the one who does everything to earn their acknowledgment."

"No, I don't expect my significant other to be a surrogate father. I want to recreate the pleasure experienced as a child, but this time in an adult male-female relationship. My father is a model for my perfect mate. The ideal man would be loving, kind, supportive, have integrity, and be faithful. He has to be well-groomed, a sharp dresser and funny. And most important, he must have faith in God, attend church regularly, and not interfere with my weekly choir practice."

"I was charmed by my second son's father. He was very muscular and intriguing. By the time I found out he was a player and not husband material, I was pregnant." Raven permitted her eyes to do the picking and didn't vet her son's father to determine if he had good character qualities.

"My first husband wooed me with kindness. He was willing to stepparent my two-year-old son. After marriage, I found out he was jealous and cheap. We had a son together and stayed married for twelve years. He was an excellent handyman and still helps me with my home repairs. He wasn't my perfect mate because our views about spending money on items I desired were different. His jealousy restricted me from interacting with people."

"Husband number two was employed, a sharp dresser, funny, liked spending time with my family, and attended church with me. He was very impressed by my home and furnishings. He invited his friends to visit and enjoyed being their tour guide. After a few months he lost interest in spending time with my family and attending church with me. My parents warned me of red flags they saw in his character. The final straw was when I found out he was cheating. When we divorced, he tried to declare my house as community property. Fortunately, according to Missouri law, he couldn't steal my assets."

Raven mirrored the mistake other women have made; she fell in love with the man her husband pretended to be.

Raven's answers to the questions on co-dependency are," I definitely and always put other's needs before mine. I have been in unhealthy relationships. I care too much about other people's opinions and judgments. I tend to overdo or work too hard. I need to control things or others in the relationship. I want to be significant. I worry a lot. I'm good at knowing what other people are doing wrong in their life. I have said yes when I want to say no."

Raven isn't co-dependent. She wants people to have a high opinion of her but her behaviors are not self-destructive. Raven is an alpha female who wants to be in control of the men in her relationship. Characteristics of the Alpha woman are she is strong, empowered, confident, successful, hard to impress, volatile when angered and high-maintenance. A dominant woman isn't reluctant to declare her desires.

Although Raven hasn't found her perfect man, she has achieved her wish to live in an upscale home with expensive furnishings. She has fulfilled her goals to have a wardrobe of beautiful clothes and accessories. Her sons are attending college, employed, and self-sufficient. As a health care professional, she earns close to six figures while helping patients with lung disease improve their breathing. She is active in her church and regularly sings in the choir. Her father's affirmation helped Raven believe she was capable of accomplishing her life's goals.

According to a recent study by the National Institute of Child Health and Human Development, "Children who receive more love from their fathers are less likely to struggle with behavioral and substance abuse problems."

Raven has witnessed the way an emotionally healthy man loves and supports his wife and children. She is on a quest to find a man with whom she can develop a similar relationship.

Update: Raven recently informed me, her Mr. Right pursued her and proposed. They plan to marry in October 2020. He has the significant characteristics of her father. She is on cloud nine.

These considerations can be valuable when selecting a partner.

Stop giving your list of requirements when you begin the relationship. Instead, observe the person's actions to determine if they fit your non-negotiable criteria.

Let him do most of the talking; he will reveal how he thinks.

Be suspicious if a man tells you early in the relationship, your wife material; especially if you've made it clear you're looking for a husband. ('Wife material' is a player statement to gain your confidence.)

Stop accepting a man at face value-consider his motives. Is he charming to disarm and manipulate you?

Does he ignore your needs in favor of his? Are there other signs of selfishness?

Is he courteous, examples: opening the door, polite, good manners?

Watch the way the person treats other people, mainly serve staff.

Create a list of 5-10 vital character qualities.

Does he encourage you to compromise your values?

Look beyond the externals of dress and grooming to the substance of the individual. Ponder Scriptural advice found in 1 Samuel 16:7," For man sees the outer appearance, but the Lord sees the heart." Player men and women capitalize on the power of presence as a magnet to attract the unsuspecting victim.

Cheryl Burton

Note the way the person handles stress, frustration, hunger, or sadness.

Do you make excuses for his bad behavior?

Compare your money philosophy and check his credit history.

How willing is the person to compromise when your opinions differ?

Do you share complementary views about a relationship with God?

If children are involved what is the person's beliefs about parenting? Are they similar or dissimilar to yours?

Check all social media posts to see how he interacts with his followers.

How does the person self-soothe-exercise, drugs, alcohol, smoking, or something else?

Do you enjoy similar types of recreation and vacation activities?

How does the person interact with their biological family and your family members?

How well does each of you connect with the other's close associates?

Consider the deeds of his friends-we tend to associate with people like us.

Does the person want to isolate you from friends and family?

Do you see signs of jealousy or excessive possessiveness?

Does the person retreat, explode or pout when angry?

What is his worldview about morality, success, right vs. wrong, etc.?

Does he envy another person's looks, success, money, or power?

No one is perfect. However, it is best to be aware of potential problem areas before you make a long-term commitment. Remember, marriage is a moral, legal, and financial obligation to another person. If you've been married you know it is much easier to enter the union than to leave it.

Reflect on your priorities. Do you gravitate to the superficial more than the substantial? If both appearance and character matter, don't settle until you have both. If truth be told, are you using another persons' appearance to make you feel valuable.?

Action Plan

List your most important factors in choosing a partner.

_____

_____

_____

_____

_____

Write the character qualities that are the most significant to you?

_____

_____

_____

_____

If you need to be in control of your relationships, list your reasons.

_____

_____

_____

_____

_____

Discuss the reasons other people's opinions matter to you.

_____

_____

_____

_____

_____

What are the ways you can improve your opinion of yourself?

_____

_____

_____

_____

_____

Chapter 4
The Substitute Father: Felicia's Story

Felicia is twenty-six with vivid memories of time spent with her biological father in early childhood. Her doe-shaped, brown eyes misted as she talked about playing with her dad in the park and at home." My dad took care of my two brothers and me while my mom worked. I was very close to my dad until my parent's divorce. He disappeared from my life after they split. My mom contacted him several times to encourage him to interact with me because I frequently cried after he left. I stayed at his house for one week but he had changed. I think he didn't feel good enough about himself or our relationship to remain a part of my life. The emotions I feel when I think about my dad, I could easily do without them. I have the capacity for an all-encompassing love, but it's for my mom. She holds herself accountable for her actions but I've lost respect for my dad."

"My mom started dating a man she later married. No one took the time to explain to me the new man would be my dad. I remember shouting at him,' you're not my dad'! But I had to go along with what they decided-I had no choice. Along with a stepfather came two stepsisters, a year older and two years younger than me. I felt jealous when I saw how hard my stepdad worked to be a part of his children's lives. My biological brothers supported one another; I had no one. I felt abandoned; my mom and I had been close before her new husband came."

"My mom and stepfather had trouble adjusting to the demands of the two families. They argued frequently and separated for several months. During the separation, my stepfather cheated and fathered a son with his ex-wife. I don't trust men in a relationship. I don't have faith in a man's ability to be grateful for what he has. My family tends to keep secrets. I don't like that practice. I think cover-ups keep you from moving forward and having a healthy connection with another person. My stepfather has a hard time accepting responsibility for his actions."

"I got in trouble a lot with my stepfather. He wanted to control everything in our lives. He monitored our phone calls; nothing was private. I didn't like the way he treated my brothers. Since I was their older sister it was my job to protect them. My stepfather and I argued and screamed at one another; we had extreme berating sessions. He called me a 'mess'. Any respect for him vanished. I felt lonely, depressed, and inadequate."

Felicia describes her stepfather as authoritarian. He practiced my house, my rules style of parenting. The only problem is that rules without relationship cause rebellion according to parenting expert Josh McDowell. Dawn Braithwaite says her research shows, "Blended families need to time develop, and that people who jump into parenting roles without first building up a rapport with their stepchildren do more harm than good." James H. Bray, former president of the American Psychological Association agrees, "If he (stepdad) tries to become too engaged in parenting before he establishes a relationship with the stepchild, the child pushes back." Joshua A. Kirsch, The Science of Stepdads.

Imagine how difficult it must have been for Felicia to lose the father she adored and have him replaced by a man she detested. She transitioned from a home of fun to one filled with conflict and control. When Felicia rebelled against her stepdads' authority, he treated it as mutiny. To maintain his power, he belittled Felicia by labeling her a 'mess.' With Felicia's self-worth assaulted she became a people- pleaser to achieve value in other people's eyes.

Another mistake Felicia's parents made was not considering the impact of the new relationship on the existing children. They were required to accept a new man in the role of the father without working through the challenges of seeing their original family dissolved. Felicia lost contact with the father she loved; a controlling, dishonest tyrant replaced him. It's no wonder she rebelled. Family therapy would have allowed the children to vent and provided the parents with useful tools to create a smooth transition into a cohesive family unit.

"As a teenager and young adult, I didn't feel smart or intelligent enough. I'm an extreme people-pleaser. I try to make people happy even if its taxing or expensive in my personal life. I will deny myself and ignore my needs in favor of satisfying others. I will process any emotions in private. I wish someone paid attention to what I need.".

"Yes, I feel physically beautiful and desirable to the opposite sex. My petite body and large butt attract a lot of men's attention. I started dating at nineteen, and that's' when I had my first sexual experience. I had planned to be a virgin until I got married. I was obsessed with my virginity. I considered myself religious, and my primary goal was to get to heaven. My stepfather gave me a purity ring as a reminder of my commitment to not having sex. I didn't have the goal of having sex. I met the guy at the water park and lost my virginity to him. I didn't feel good enough or emotionally intelligent enough. He cheated on me."

"I fear getting too close in a relationship. I also think I find it easy to fall in love. I relish the idea of love, but I'm not prepared to deal with the heartbreak. I behaved like a thirsty woman with my first boyfriend. I thought about him continuously. I stalked him on the Internet. I was too accessible and frequently texted him. He' gaslighted' me attempting to make me think I was crazy and overreactive. I felt like he was judging and attacking me. I learned on Valentine's day that he messaged his ex-girlfriend on Instagram. I thought we were exclusive. I blocked him after that for one year. I wish the act of loving someone didn't hurt."

Felicia has had dissatisfying experiences with the men in her life; the three men she relied on for love and affirmation disappointed her. However, her previous relationships don't have to define her life. She can invest in deep self-understanding and improve her self-esteem. She can learn healthy methods to satisfy her emotional needs.

Felicia is an example to other people on how to treat her. Before expecting other people's approval, she needs to love herself. It starts with Felicia's mindset. She has to remove the negative labels placed on her by other people and replace them with tags that extoll her worth.

Felicia can declare I love me and resolve to be my best friend. I am worthy of being treated with courtesy and respect. I will be honest and trustworthy with you and I require your honesty and trustworthiness in return. I choose not to deceive you in big or small ways. If you cannot honor me our relationship will end. I commit to improving my self-love, self-trust, self-awareness, and integrity. I accept I am a work in progress and commit to my self-growth. I will learn the lessons offered by my past relationships. I will examine them with a microscope and consider what I did right and what I did wrong that needs to improve. I will forgive myself for compromising my values to please another person. I forgive myself for devaluing me and accepting without question another person's view of my worth. I believe I deserve the romantic relationship I want and refuse to settle for less. I require peace and happiness in life. I have a God-given purpose in my life that I will achieve.

While it can be painful to expose the truth about yourself, an aspect of improving self-awareness is to tell yourself the truth.

If Felicia takes time to reflect on the reasons the major men in her life failed, she'll become more aware of the signs this type of man displays. She'll recognize the red flags. Knowledge will enable her to attract the man with the character, morals, and integrity of her dreams and repel the others. If Felicia requires professional help to improve herself, she can invest in a life coach or mental health specialist.

Felicia is confident about her career choice. She is studying to be an esthetician and plans to become an expert in eyebrow tattooing and own a beauty salon.

For further self-improvement answer the following questions:

What are the reasons for your poor self-esteem?

_____

_____

_____

_____

_____

List ways you will improve your self-worth.

_____

_____

_____

_____

_____

List the most important characteristics for your future mate.

_____

_____

_____

_____

_____

Why did you play small and weak in your relationships?

_____

_____

_____

_____

_____

Review what you did to receive love in previous relationships. What will you change? What behavior will you commit to never repeating?

_____

_____

_____

_____

_____

What can you do to improve your relationship with your stepfather?

_____

_____

_____

_____

_____

Chapter 5
The Work-a-holic Father: Ruth's Story

Some psychologists claim that workaholism is an addiction similar to drugs or alcohol. The afflicted person spends long hours at work and neglects family and friends. Not everyone agrees that workaholism is negative. Ruth says," my father worked a lot. He often had two jobs but he cared for me."

"My grandfather died when my dad was in high school. My dad dropped out of school and became the primary breadwinner for the family. He learned early that a man provides for the people he loves."

"My earliest memory was of my dad feeding me. He hugged me and told me he loved me. I was daddy's little girl. He was warm and loving towards me. I felt safe. He was a good provider. He gave me the two things I loved, money for candy and pretty clothes to wear. I remember him giving my mom money for us to go shopping for clothing. My sister and I participated in dance class and school plays. My dad attended when he could. I am the oldest daughter and the one who looks the most like him. I was fortunate to inherit the best features of my mom and dad. My dad told me I was pretty and as I matured other guys did too."

"I started dating at fourteen and having sex at fifteen. There wasn't any real thought behind it-I just liked it. The person I was dating wanted sex and I wanted to please him. I didn't feel pressured. I had my first son at eighteen and the second at twenty-two. My dad didn't say much but my mom was angry and disappointed. My dad didn't discuss how a man should treat me, relationships, or sex. I think many daughters would have been uncomfortable with the topic." Linda Nielson, Ph.D., Institute for Family Studies says, "most daughters also wish their fathers talked with them more about sex and relationships even though the conversation would have been uncomfortable at first."

"I demanded respect and refused to be with a man who didn't honor me. I don't tolerate cheating or disrespect."

"I am an introvert and a loner. As a child, I felt fearful and anxious in crowds. I tend to withdraw around a lot of people. I don't need a man in my life to function. I'm okay being by myself. I was married for three years. We had one son together. It didn't work out and we divorced. I will work on a relationship until I see it can't work. Now I'm living with a man."

"I think a good relationship with a dad encourages a woman to seek intimate fulfilling relationships rather than settling for what's less than satisfying. I will give a man several chances before I exit."

Ruth responded to the co-dependency questions with, "I tend to put other's needs before mine and I like to make sure everyone is okay. For a genuine need I will give the shirt off my back but I won't buy a man things to keep him.

Ruth says," I lean towards overdoing or working too hard similar to my hard-working father. I'm in the middle about boundaries; they're neither too tight or too loose. I enjoy being needed by my guy; I don't make it so he needs me all the time. I'm pretty good at knowing what other people are doing wrong in their life. I have said yes when I want to say no,"

Ruth never behaved as a thirsty woman. Ruth's dad's demonstration of love and acceptance boosted her self-esteem and enhanced her sense of being valuable. A father is a substantial role model. Without using words, he taught Ruth self-belief and to demand respect in an interpersonal relationship. He also modeled the worthiness of working to achieve a dream. Ruth's story suggests that quality time spent with a daughter can help her become a strong woman who doesn't experience father hunger or codependency.

Ruth is forty-eight, pretty, and still in her prime. But a day is coming when Ruth's earthly life will end and her decision about where she will spend eternity looms large. Her father taught her to be successful in life and to work hard to attain dreams. He didn't challenge her to consider where she would spend eternity. According to 2 Corinthians 5:10, in the New International Version (NIV) bible, "We must all appear before the judgment seat of Christ that each one may receive what is due us for the things done in the body whether good or bad." Ruth has a heavenly father who is affectionately called Abba either meaning daddy or Father. And like any earthly father, God requires specific standards of behavior. The difference is that those who don't meet Gods' standards and haven't received Jesus Christ as Savior spend eternity apart from Him in eternal torment, aka Hell. Each person must decide whether they accept the previous statement as accurate. A Bible fact check will confirm this information.

Ruth has a dual career as a massage therapist and a barber. Her two jobs keep her busy at work like her dad.

"My dad died eleven years ago. I feel sad because he isn't here. He had a dry sense of humor. I miss him."

Action Plan

Write the reasons other people's needs are more important than yours.

_____

_____

_____

_____

How do you explain saying yes when you want to say no?

_____

_____

_____

_____

List the ways you manage anxiety in crowds. What can you improve? What can you eliminate?

_____

_____

_____

_____

How does overwork fulfill you?

_____

_____

_____

_____

_____

Chapter 6
Another View of a Workaholic Dad: Faith's Story

"My dad worked long hours. He had two jobs. If I summed up my dads' expectations it would be to have the family without the work. Children were a testimony to his manhood. He had two sons and two daughters. My dad justified his long hours away from the family with the excuse it would enable him to buy the house my mom desired. It never happened. His conversation was always about work and the promise of a new home purchase- his explanation for working hard. He provided food, clothing, and shelter. He would give us candy but the sweets were a bribe to leave him alone.

According to Workaholic Anonymous, the signs of a workaholic are the person is more excited about work than anything else. Most of their conversations are work-related. The long hours hurt personal relationships. The workaholic believes more money will solve other problems in life.

Compare the description of a workaholic with Faith's story of her relationship with her dad.

"I don't recall much about my family life before the age of ten. This information described our relationship when I was ten until high school age. It was detached and nonchalant. My dad gave me candy to get rid of me. I wanted my dad to be involved in my life and understanding of my challenges. I was able to communicate with him better as I grew older. Sometimes I could talk to him and other times he seemed distant. When he picked me up from work, and we rode home together, he asked, 'How is school; do you need any money? He frequently said, 'I'm working hard to get us a house.' The conversations were fluff-school or his job at work. Dad never asked about me as a person."

"I remember my dad telling me to be quiet. Maybe it was because I was the family tattle-tale; I revealed what my older brother and sister did. Their payback was to double-team me. My dads' discipline was to say, 'don't do it again'; he never spanked me. Dad was not loving or directional. I was lonely for his affection. I never sat on his lap or was consoled by him. He was emotionally unavailable to me but not to my older sister. I watched her for clues on how to interact with him. I was fearful of my older brother and sister. I felt like I was on the outside looking in where I observed my mom pay more attention to my sister. Maybe if I could grow up faster, I wouldn't have to see my parents focusing more on my sister than me. I believed I should hurry up and learn what I needed to and move out. My dad would sit and eat and the only talking he did was about his business or his truck with his eyes closed."

"I don't know a lot about my dad's family because he didn't introduce them to us nor did we visit them."

Faith recalled bittersweet memories of she and her sister attending private school." I felt stereotyped because there were only five black students in the entire school. My dad didn't appear at my eighth-grade graduation; it was my big day, but it wasn't significant to him. I improved my self-esteem by learning to compete mentally. I would drill myself to expand my skills. I wasn't a sore loser. I wanted to learn how to get better."

"In adolescence, I had bad acne with red bumps all over my face. I wore braces. I wasn't overweight, but guys never complimented me on my figure. I wasn't interested in guys until high school. I was more concerned about my education. I was a junior in high school when I met the first boy I wanted to date-he was two years older."

"When I was in high school, I wanted my dad present, but by then, he and my mom had separated. I saw him even less after they split. I made sure he received an invitation to my high school graduation but he didn't come. I teared up and was angry that he didn't see me graduate. He didn't give me an excuse for not being there. I resented him. I put my dad on a pedestal when talking about him to my friends to ward off questions. I wanted my mom and dad to rekindle their marriage. I loved my mom and wanted that love to spill over to dad."

"My oldest brother and my uncle were my role-models growing up. They served as a substitute dad."

"I saw my dad several years after he had left our family and started a new one. By then he had separated from the other woman. He was sick and recovering from a stroke. He wanted to reconnect with our family. I was instrumental in helping him spend time with us at family gatherings. His memories of my childhood were different from mine. He said I was a daddy's girl-his baby girl. I was the one who didn't cause him problems. He claimed he bragged about me and was proud that I was in the Upward Bound program. He never told me I was pretty. He was impressed by my academic achievements."

"I started dating at seventeen; I was too clingy. I fell in love fast. My first sexual experience was at seventeen. I got pregnant with my first son. I could read a guy and know when he was cheating. I nursed persistent thoughts about how to get even when a man wounded me. I did stalk the man and imagined doing something hurtful to retaliate and cause him pain. My most embarrassing activity was the time I waited for my man to take a shower and hacked his cell-phone to learn about the girl he was seeing. I confronted her. He and I went to her house. My revenge was that he didn't end up with either one of us."

"Yes, I did undesirable sexual acts to hold a man. I wanted to have a family with children. I dreamed of being a stay at home mom with twin girls and one boy. I had three sons without the man. When the man I cared about told me he was only with his wife for the children. I realized I couldn't do anything to satisfy him; I could see things were going downhill so I left. Everything was all about him; I was angry at being used. Unfortunately, I have tolerated verbal abuse but I don't accept cheating."

"I am self-confident and satisfied with my femininity and competence. I am very organized and make sure I record all critical facts. Some consider me an alpha female. I am a leader. I sit in the driver's seat; I am strong, independent, I know what I want and how to get it. My desire to take over and be in control originated in childhood; I wanted to be free.

This quote from Quotes.com applies to Faith. 'It is my nature to be kind, gentle, and loving. But know this: When it comes to matters of protecting my friends, my family and my heart do not trifle with me for I am the most powerful and relentless creature you'll ever know.'

"Someone can suggest but I may not listen, because I know I want to be in control. I have to be certain everything is okay. I may have a little OCD (Obsessive Compulsive Disorder). Even after going to bed I get up to check the stove to make sure it's turned off and the doors to ensure they are locked. I still have trust issues. In my earlier life lots of guys did me wrong and hurt me; I didn't like it. I hold grudges, especially at work. I don't like someone lying about me. I'm not going to lie; no one is that special that I would lie about them."

In my marriage when my husband criticizes me-I go with the flow. I'm mostly happy in my marriage because with my dad not being emotionally present, I learned to self-nurture.

Faith answers the codependency questions with," no, I don't put others' needs before mine. I don't stay in unhealthy relationships. Sometimes, I'm too aggressive. I don't care about other people's opinions and judgments. I keep boundaries so tight they could be considered rigid. I need to be in charge. Someone needing me isn't necessary. But sometimes I get confused about what my needs are and frustrated with other people who don't meet them. I worry a lot. To a certain extent, I am good at knowing what other people are doing wrong with their life. I have said yes when I wanted to say no." Codependency is not an issue for Faith.

Faith is a Pharmacy Technician. She occasionally works as a certified nurse assistant (CNA), providing private duty home care services.

Action Plan

Explain the reasons you need to be in control.

_____

_____

_____

_____

_____

What are the disadvantages of maintaining control?

_____

_____

_____

_____

_____

What are your chief worries; how do you manage them?

_____

_____

_____

_____

_____

List your primary needs. How do you fulfill them?

_____

_____

_____

_____

_____

What are the reasons you don't share your desires with your intimates?

_____

_____

_____

_____

_____

What are your motives when you say yes when you want to say no?

_____

_____

_____

_____

_____

Chapter 7
The Uninvolved Father: Betty's story

"If your presence doesn't make an impact, then your absence won't make a difference."

Unknown

At fourteen, Betty is the youngest contributor. "Betty said, "My relationship with my father was on and off and unhealthy. Communication between us rarely occurred; if we did talk, he mostly lied. He made promises he didn't keep; for example, dad said he would buy me a pair of shoes. I haven't seen them yet. My opinion didn't matter; when he did buy me clothes, he bought items he liked. I think it was a form of manipulation. His common excuse was, 'My girlfriend will get it for you or, I can't do that now; I'll do it later.' But later never came. I don't trust him with anything now. I stopped believing him when I realized he didn't know how to be a father. I met his father and I know that my father didn't have a good role model."

"My mom has been my father figure. She provided things my father should have. It would have been better if someone of a different gender also helped; not having a father to support and guide me has damaged my self-esteem. I control the loneliness I feel for a father by telling myself I don't care. I feel attractive to the opposite sex; boys say I'm fly. I'm self-confident in my femininity. My family assures me I am competent, and my mom inspires me to do the right things. Sometimes I feel rage and I bump my head into a wall. My mom says the anger comes from my dad's side of the family; my uncle and grandfather demonstrated violent anger. Sometimes I smoke marijuana and drink alcohol. My psychiatrist told me marijuana could damage my brain, decrease my concentration, and affect my ability to think. I don't date but I occasionally hang out with guys and girlfriends. No sex for me yet. I feel a lot of emotions like depression, nervousness, fear but mostly fury when I think about my dad. His actions infuriate me especially when I see and hear the way he talks to my mom. Sometimes I have an excessive need to feel valued. I hesitate to get too close to a person because of potential pain. I am afraid of being rejected by my mom, dad, sister, granny, and aunt. I don't believe I am a thirsty girl but I haven't been in a real relationship yet. I know what a thirsty girl acts like and I don't plan to be that person."

Betty has listed some of the problems a girl with an uninvolved father experience. Researchers agree with Betty's conclusions. They determined that this neglectful parent often provided the bare minimum the child needed for physical comfort and emotional sustenance. Hugging, kissing, and emotional support were absent. Betty missed the pleasure of non-sexual touching by a father. Any physical affection had to be provided by the mother or other family members. This adolescent girl learned to manage any loneliness for her dad without adult intervention. Ineffective communication with her dad deprived Betty of the opportunity to learn to express her desires to a caring man.

Negotiating for needs is often discovered in the biological family. Fathers play an essential role in the daughter's development of self-worth. When he confirms her value in his eyes the daughter feels more substantial. At least by seeing a psychiatrist, Betty has a venue in which she can express her frustrations and have a guide on the road to recovery.

Dr. Charles Stanley, A Father's Influence, In Touch Magazine, says, "the uninvolved or absent father sends the message that his children are unimportant and both he and God are too busy for them." Betty disagrees, she says her mom models a strong belief in God and assures Betty that God loves her and can provide the psychological and spiritual support she needs. In this case, Betty's father's error doesn't mean she believes God has abandoned her.

On their site, The National Society for Prevention of Cruelty to Children, (NSPCC.og., 2020) states," neglected children take risks like running away from home and using drugs and alcohol. These children display a higher incidence of mental health problems like depression and Attention Deficit Hyperactivity Disorder (ADHD)" Betty has run away from home, used drugs and alcohol, experienced depression and bouts of anger."

"My dad was furious when he heard I had run away and stayed gone for several days. The guys we were with stole a car." My dad yelled, 'you and your sister are doing the very things that sent me to prison.' "It was a scary experience that I won't repeat. My guy friends told my sister and me to go home-you have a good mama who cares about you."

Maybe her dad is starting to see the importance of his guidance and direction in Betty's life.

As Betty matures will she be tempted to find a spouse who supplies what she missed in her dad? Perhaps, some women do. Will only emotionally unavailable men pique Betty's interest because of familiarity with that type of relationship? That has happened as well. Will distrust be Betty's default position because of fractured trust in her dads' word? Will Betty wear an impenetrable armor to prevent a person from getting too close? Betty has the advantage of seeking understanding at an early age. Her insight into the connection between her dad's poor parenting and the deficit he experienced can help her develop compassion and forgiveness. It's a challenge for someone to give what they haven't received. Another plus is Betty's mom and extended family who love and support her.

Betty has plans to become a doctor; she hasn't chosen the specialty yet. She is leaning towards Pediatrics. Betty makes good grades. She sees a psychiatrist to help manage her anger and discuss her feelings.

Action Plan

List the activities you enjoy that make you feel worthwhile.

_____

_____

_____

_____

_____

What did you learn when you ran away from home?

_____

_____

_____

_____

What character qualities will you look for in a mate?

_____

_____

_____

_____

_____

What are the disadvantages of being a single parent mom?

_____

_____

_____

_____

_____

Which self-improvement activities will you practice to help achieve your professional and personal goals?

_____

_____

_____

_____

_____

Chapter 8
The Divorced Dad: Jo's story

"Some dads teach a daughter who not to choose."

Cheryl Burton

"My dad left our family when I was ten. He wanted the other woman. Before that, life was good when he was around. He was playful, kind, and loved the outdoors. He would take us fishing. Dad was an over the road truck driver. I was used to his absence for long periods. When he was home mom and dad argued a lot. One day, after being gone, he showed up at the door, he didn't stay long. Our life changed because he and mom divorced. We became poorer than before. We weren't a family who discussed things. My mom had eight pregnancies and lost three full-term babies. There were five girls left. My mom was tired and hard to be around. Kids develop resentment. Occasionally my dad returned and took us fishing."

"I was born in a small town in southern Illinois with a population of six thousand. Divorce was very rare in the late 1950's. Divorce was a social taboo." Only 2.6 people out of 1,000 divorced according to 1950's Family Life. "I felt embarrassed because of my parent's divorce. I didn't know any other divorced parents. I was ashamed that my third-grade teacher who grew up with my mom also knew about the divorce."

When Jo was young, she struggled with humiliation for two reasons, her poverty, and her parents' divorce. Her immature mind said there is something wrong with you because of your parent's choices. Jo joins the other women in the book whose shame says there is something wrong with who you are.

"When I was in the fifth grade, my mom served school lunches- she saw some kids smoking. That prompted mom to lecture me about not smoking, not using bad language and, how to act like a lady." Jo's mom set the standard for conduct in the home.

"In the sixth- grade dad kidnapped me and I lived with him and his girlfriend in a small apartment in town. Two of my sisters also lived with us for a year. The other sisters stayed with my mom. Dad married his girlfriend; she was twelve years older than him. It wasn't a bad situation. My stepmom was a decent cook, and she made our clothes. At the end of the summer of that same year, my mom took us back. She had legal custody. I was angry because my mom kidnapped me. I left again at the first opportunity. My sister gave me the dollar I needed for a bus ticket. I hopped the bus and ran away to live with dad. My mom called the sheriff and he took me back home; this time, I stayed. My mom remarried a Christian. My stepdad took me to church; he complimented me, praised me for my grades, and encouraged me to do my best."

"My third sister married as a teenager to escape. Unfortunately, the Vietnam war took her husband's life. She remarried for money six months later. She didn't know he was her half-brother, a narcissist, controller, and gambler who stole her money and kept her a prisoner. She remained married to him for thirty-nine years. She is one example of the chaos and domino effect the family experienced after my parents' divorce."

"My father was an atheist with no understanding of God. Dad called me weird because I believed in God and went to church. I hoped dad would accept Jesus as his Savior when he developed colon cancer in his seventies, but he didn't. He wasn't horrible; he was well-liked and very bright. My mother was a Christian and established the family's morals. Around the house, mom sang old hymns. She sent us to church but never attended. When I accepted the Lord Jesus, my life felt different. I enjoyed singing at church every Sunday but felt uncomfortable because I always wore the same dress. I thought people looked down on me because I had few clothes.

"In his fifty's my dad still partied. Wife number three was a gambler. Their marriage lasted twenty-three years. In total dad was married fifty-eight years. I don't think he was immoral, just selfish. Dad was a womanizer who did whatever suited him, including leaving his family. I didn't want to marry a man like my father."

Jo later learned information about her parents that could explain their behavior. "She said, "my paternal controlling grandfather wouldn't permit my dad to attend college. My mother was pregnant when they married. She remained emotionally unavailable and unexpressive to her children. Her main problem was unforgiveness." Did her mom and dad resent not being able to fulfill their dreams?

"When I was a junior in high school I rarely dated. I wanted a trustworthy, honest person who didn't cuss or smoke. I had a healthy fear of sex outside of marriage; I didn't want to get pregnant, plus I didn't have a lot of sexual urges. I was an 'A' student but I had low self-esteem. I was five feet tall and chubby without cute clothes. I had to make do; for instance, I tied my poorly-fitting shirt up with a rope. I worked as a carhop at a fast food place to earn cash. My mom couldn't take me to school events so I didn't go. I believed my school mates ostracized me. But I was also shy and didn't engage because I felt socially unacceptable. My low self-worth and discomfort about our poverty kept people from visiting our home. The neighbors in a two-block perimeter around our home were as impoverished as us. When I was home, I worked around the house and played with my siblings."

My first date at seventeen took me to the prom. When the guy got fresh by putting his hands where they didn't belong, I refused to go out with him again. My other dates were church-related. I spent time with a guy on and off for three years. He kept pressuring me for sex but he said he'd never give me a ring. He lived in a trailer while in college. One night he spiked my drink and we ended up in bed. I asked if he loved me and he said he wasn't the marrying kind. I believe I was in a co-dependent relationship. I didn't have the strength to break it off. I felt depressed, nervous, and fearful. When I looked down the road, all I saw was blankness. I prayed about the relationship and asked God to help me break-up with him and eventually, I did."

"The Navigators Christian Ministry taught me biblical principles. In a bible study I learned about the sovereignty of God over my life. I reflected on how to apply God's teachings. I concluded I needed to forgive and love my parents. I became more affectionate towards them. I eliminated the resentment toward my mother for her distance and disinterest in my life. I abolished the bitterness against my father for leaving our family and for being selfish and ungodly."

"Although I wasn't physically attracted to my husband, his character impressed me, especially his maturity in Christ. We raised emotionally and psychologically healthy children and share a love for Jesus Christ. We attend church and enjoy spending time with our grandchildren. I am a retired elementary school teacher."

Jo preferred to live with her dad rather than her mom. The evidence is her escape plan to return to him. Jo's dad modeled being a womanizer, unfaithful in marriage, playful, kind, a nature lover, and devoid of faith in God. She didn't mention that dad affirmed her value or paid attention to her accomplishments. Jo elected not to marry a man like her dad. She chose a man of substance who represented integrity, character, honor, and trustworthiness. Note her husband embodied qualities similar to those of her stepfather. Her stepdad took Jo to church, provided stability, and encouraged her to strive for academic excellence. According to Bill Muehlenberg,

Dads and Daughters' Fact Sheet, August 2014, "many studies show a close connection between fatherly affirmation and a woman's self-esteem, fear of intimacy, comfort with womanhood and comfort with sexuality." Jo is fortunate that her stepdad provided what her dad didn't.

Jo's involvement with a boyfriend who spoke his truth also helped her decide who she wanted for a partner. She resolved not to chase a man who told her, 'I'm not the marrying kind, and I will not give you a ring.' For a brief time, her hunger for affection dulled her hearing but she self-corrected and focused on her spiritual growth. That decision yielded Jo a stable marriage and a satisfying relationship with her grandchildren. Note, Jo chose a man of substance over flash.

At seventy-one Jo has learned how to be psychologically content. She has forgiven her mom and dad for their failures. Her decision to forgive is a powerful witness of God's love. Instead of resentment and bitterness which can repel and broadcast a negative message, love can improve receptivity to the gospel teachings. Unforgiveness offers a false sense of power that keeps rage and resentment alive. After Jo explored her parent's family history, she accepted that her parents couldn't provide her what they never received.

Chapter 9
Betrayer Dad: Eva's Story

"Each betrayal begins with trust."

Martin Luther

"I was four when my dad left. I loved him and thought he loved me. No one told me the reason he disappeared. Our family didn't talk about tough subjects. Occasionally dad contacted my mom and promised he'd visit but he was a no-call and no show. I'd dress and eagerly wait for a dad who never came. Although my mom appeared angry, we never talked about the reason for dads' behavior. She eventually stopped telling me he was coming. At age ten he promised to buy me a pair of shoes; instead of taking me shopping he sent his girlfriend. She gave me an old pair of worn-out shoes. I don't know if my dad knew about it; all I know is I experienced disappointment after disappointment."

I label Eva's dad a betrayer because he violated the trust, she had in him. He lied to her and hurt her by maximizing his needs and minimizing hers. Dishonesty cracks the foundation of a daughter's belief system and is the highest betrayal in a relationship. If a parent is untrustworthy the believability of other people suffers too.

"My sister's husband occasionally babysat my brother and me. He began molesting me when I was seven; the abuse continued for two years. He would put me on a couch and fondle my vagina and lick his fingers. Sometimes, I'd pretend to be asleep. My three-year-old brother was an occasional witness. The abuser warned me not to tell anyone; he said they wouldn't believe me and my sister would stop loving me. Once he chased me around the house with an erection though I didn't know what it was at the time. All I know is I was scared. When another adult returned, my abuser grinned and said, 'I'll be back.' Even though I felt upset I stayed silent."

Eva experienced a second betrayal of trust. Her brother-in-law pretended to be a concerned caregiver, and instead, he violated Eva, his wife, and his mother-in-law's trust. He used fear to intimidate and encourage Eva's silence. His behavior reinforced Eva's belief that her world was an unsafe place and, men hurt rather than cherished her.

"When my mom remarried my stepfather said my dad was unwelcome at his house. My stepfather became an unwanted father figure. He was very moody especially when he came home from work. He had one gray eye and one brown eye. When tired or angry his gray eye changed to black, and instead of talking, he'd grunt. My mom paced and spoke softly. Mom said, 'I'm afraid he won't give me any money for household expenses; we must be careful not to upset him.' I walked on eggshells and avoided interacting with him. My childhood was a very confusing time in my life. My stepfather treated my stepsister, his biological daughter, kindly. He sang to her and rocked her to sleep when she was a toddler. He often said,' give the baby what she wants.'

My stepfather provided me food, clothing, and a decent place to live but no hugs, kisses, or praise. Why didn't I deserve to be comforted? I felt lonely and abandoned by my dad and tolerated by my stepdad. I didn't see dad again until I was sixteen. The meeting was painful and didn't repair our broken relationship. Since childhood I've developed a void in my soul that has never gone away."

Did Eva's mom implicitly betray her? Eva flashed signals of sorrow from losing the relationship with her dad and envy of her stepdad's treatment of his daughter. Her sexual molestation by her brother-in-law remained undetected by her mom. Implicit is being capable of understanding something, even if it is unexpressed. Is it reasonable to expect a busy mom to be a detective? Perhaps Eva's moms' struggles managing her marital relationship blinded her to Eva's needs. In the ideal world a parent honors the requirements of the child. If the demands are undiscovered the child develops the kinds of maladaptive coping patterns Eva did.

"Fear stalked me as a child. I felt unprotected. I didn't have any friends or family with whom I could talk. I lay in bed at night, and the shadows on the wall were monsters. In my youth I didn't feel attractive. I thought of myself as fat and ugly."

"I started experimenting with sex at thirteen mostly because of curiosity. My body developed early and men complimented me and called me luscious. I felt powerful knowing I could control them with sexual desire. My first sexual partner's uncle gave us condoms to use. I started dating at seventeen and using drugs and alcohol to relieve the emotional hurts. I feared getting too close in a relationship because of probable anguish. I expected to be rejected by men because I felt inadequate."

"During a short period, I dressed like a man; I wore men's clothes. I wanted to be seen as strong so that people wouldn't hurt me."

"I met my first husband at seventeen. I was with a group of girls when he approached and asked, 'which one of you wants to go out with me?' "I stepped forward and said,' I do.' We married when I turned eighteen. My stepfather warned me I was making a mistake. He told me to fulfill my dream of attending nursing school instead and he'd pay the bill. I didn't listen. I needed to get out of that house. I made a huge mistake. My husband was physically and verbally abusive. He sodomized me on our wedding night. I was too proud to return home and admit I made a mistake. My husband was ten years older and couldn't read and didn't want me to either. I'd hide a book in the dirty clothes and studied while I washed them. My husband was an IV drug user who started drinking alcohol at four. Life with him was hell-but I stayed and had one child. I had frequent panic attacks and felt very nervous. I finally divorced him after six years."

"My second husband was a verbally, abusive alcoholic. We raised three children; two were our biological daughters plus the daughter from my first marriage. Chaos and disagreements were our relationship companions. I continued to select men who treated me the way I felt about myself. My self-esteem was in the basement and worthless haunted my mind. I endured this marriage for sixteen years. We divorced after I discovered his cheating."

In my fifties I don't feel attractive. I don't like the way I look. I deliberately gain weight to hide my inferiority. When I'm fat I hate to look at myself. I'm weary of weight loss programs and going to the gym to exercise. Even when I was thin with a pretty body, I didn't value myself."

"There have been periods in my life that I behaved as a thirsty woman. I engaged in humiliating activities; I performed undesirable sex acts to hold onto a man; I've been more upset than happy in a relationship and often felt lonely; I tolerated physical, emotional, and psychological abuse, and I tried to control my partners behaviors."

Eva's father introduced her to betrayal; Eva added hurt, unhappiness, and low self-confidence. The other significant people in her life picked up the ball and ran with it. Each person cemented her core belief of valuelessness. Her brother-in-law taught that her body was for his pleasure without her consent. To keep her silent the brother-in-law magnified her fear of rejection if she told of the abuse. Her mother didn't explain her father's absence or inform her husband of a girl's need for non-sexual physical affection and emotional connection. Her mother taught Eva to keep family secrets. Her stepfather demonstrated emotional unavailability and ignored her need for approval and validation. Both of her husbands provided unique forms of betrayal and reinforced Eva's belief she deserved poor treatment. Eva betrayed herself by making bad decisions and labeling herself as unworthy of honor, trust, and genuine caring.

Fortunately, Eva has become dedicated to self-growth. Despite the betrayals, despite the rejections by herself and others, Eva accomplished noteworthy goals. Eva chose not to wallow in pain. She completed her nursing education and is a nursing supervisor. Eva reached her main professional goal but her personal goals need fine-tuning. She is achieving self-understanding and learning to eliminate negative self-appraisal with the assistance of a counselor. She is mastering body acceptance and altering what she doesn't like. The only males in her intimate circle are her grandsons and her faithful dog. Eva needs to love herself before attempting to love another person. She is developing her spiritual self and using biblical principles as her template.

Action Plan

List all the reasons you love yourself.

_____

_____

_____

_____

_____

What are your primary strengths?

_____

_____

_____

_____

_____

What is the purpose of your life?

_____

_____

_____

_____

_____

Cheryl Burton

Who do you need to forgive?

_____

_____

_____

_____

_____

List the ways you will take care of your body.

_____

_____

_____

_____

_____

What are healthy ways you will manage loneliness?

_____

_____

_____

_____

_____

Which negative words do you say about yourself? How do you mitigate them?

_____

_____

_____

_____

_____

Chapter 10
Distant Dad: Melba's Story

A distant dad can be physically present yet uninvolved in a daughter's life. Melba describes the relationship with her dad as remote. "I would see him occasionally when I was under eight years old. Although he moved in with my mother and me when I was over eight, I still only saw him infrequently. My dad was an alcoholic and an OG, an old gangster. I remember a time when my dad and mom argued and he hit her. I jumped on his back and began punching him. I had some of his violent behavior in me." Melba's aggressive behavior fueled her life and enabled her to remain steadfast in achieving her goals.

"I feel disappointed when I think about my dad and his side of the family. Dad was an engineer, very witty, and a sound businessman. Yet his business failed because of alcoholism. My father never knew his father. I never interacted with my paternal grandmother because she didn't believe I was his child."

According to some experts' people who experienced poor parenting become emotionally distant. To cope with their pain and sorrow they turn to liquid support from alcohol. Not knowing his dad and seeing his mother reject his daughter must have been difficult for Melbas' dad.

"My childhood best friend's father served as a father figure. He was very interested in my life. I took to heart his many teachings which helped to shape who I am today. Her father challenged me to seek an education beyond high school. He was an EMT (Emergency Medical Technician) and an M.D. (Medical Doctor). While his daughter avoided listening to her father, I embraced his involvement. No one else talked to me about going to college. I didn't receive recognition and encouragement from very many other people. I had to learn self-motivation."

"I only missed my father when I saw the dynamic and intimate relationship between other children and their fathers. My mother compensated for my father's detachment by being very interested and directive in my life."

"I never felt truly lonely. I am an only child and an introvert. I found joy in being alone; I read, sang, drew, colored, and wrote poetry. I felt fearful as a child when I considered what might happen to me if my mother died. I didn't want to have to stay with another relative or my father. If I were old enough, I would have been on my own."

"My self-confidence bloomed by being a model. I was tall growing up and 5'10" as an adult. I learned to carry myself with dignity and grace and to dress to accentuate my body 's best features. I have always felt confident and attractive. I draw men's attention and, some of them 'hit on' me, which reassures me I am desirable. I love being a woman and all the benefits that come with it. I admit I have leveraged my beauty to influence decisions in professional and personal relationships. I am very determined. When someone tells me, I can't do something I find a way to prove them wrong. I am naturally able to achieve most of what I set out to do."

"I began dating at 13-14. My first sexual experience was at 17-18. I had sex for three reasons; love, curiosity, and he told me I was the girl he wanted to marry. This decent guy and I were a couple for four years but we didn't marry. I have had some bad relationships but mostly good ones. I am strong-willed but willing to compromise within reason. I feel competent and self-assured. I have never indulged in self-injurious behavior like cutting, using drugs or alcohol. I avoided alcohol because I didn't want to be like my father."

"I married at 19 to escape the memories of my abusive father. I was vulnerable, frustrated, and angry with my dad. The man I married was tall, dark, handsome, well-educated, articulate, strong and confident like my father. We dated for six months. I didn't want my husband to serve as a surrogate father because I don't like someone telling me what to do. My husband became physically and emotionally abusive during the one month we were married. I left him after three weeks. I picked up the pieces and began dating again. I dated one man for six years. He was a closet racist who looked bi-racial. He resented his relatives for their treatment of his bi-racial mother. Our relationship didn't endure. Thirteen years after my marriage ended, I met another guy who fathered my daughter. We never married."

"Sometimes, I blame or dislike myself because my partner doesn't fulfill my emotional and psychological needs."

"Almost three years ago I married a man who had been a friend for several years. We met while working together. I know his work ethic and he knows mine. We have similar work interests. He is a supervisor for a computer company and I am an Information Technology (I.T.) Project Manager professional and a college professor. We both had been married before and knew some of the challenges of marriage. He has three children so I became an instant mother of four. He relentlessly pursued me until I agreed to date and then marry him. We are building a life and a consulting business."

In response to the questions on co-dependency, Melba said," I do tend to put the needs of my mother, husband, and child before mine. I want to be needed. It's good to know people want me around. I only desire to control myself not things or people. I don't believe I care too much about other peoples' opinion. I'm not too passive or aggressive in relationships. I can be rigid but I'm working on balancing my boundaries. I do tend to overdo or work too hard. I know I use work as an escape. Sometimes I worry a lot. I'm usually good at knowing what other people are doing wrong in their life. Their behavior confirms my intuition. I don't recall saying yes when I wanted to say no,"

Melba does not appear to be co-dependent. She seems to have a healthy self-respect and self-confidence. Her answers don't indicate self-destructive behaviors.

Melba answered yes to one thirsty woman question. She acknowledged being more upset than happy in her first marriage. Remember, their union lasted three weeks. She refused to be a volunteer victim or to tolerate abuse.

Melba used wisdom in agreeing to marry her second husband. Unlike with her first husband, she assessed husband number two's track record and determined his essential character qualities. Melba's husband didn't appear to have the characteristics of her distant father. Instead, he had the mental and moral assets she admired. They share faith in Jesus Christ, attend church together, and sing in the choir. They are improving their leadership and speaking skills as Toastmasters. Melba and her husband are committed to dynamic personal and professional growth. They share common professional interests and want to build a business and a life. Melba observed his connection and interaction with his biological children. One of her primary concerns was to protect her teenage daughter from a harmful influence. Melba's daughter didn't oppose their marriage.

Action Plan

List the reasons you choose work as an escape.

_____

_____

_____

_____

_____

How do you manage your chief worries?

_____

_____

_____

_____

_____

Chapter 11
Neglectful Dad: Alice's Story

"Dad- I feel lost without you"

Cheryl Burton

Alice admits," I don't know my dad. He was in my life from birth to five years old. My mom said he was an alcoholic. My most reliable memory was of him whipping me one time. He and my mom divorced after she discovered he cheated and fathered a daughter outside of the marriage. As a child I didn't see my father although I've heard he attempted to reconcile with my sister and me. My mother was very angry with him and prevented his interaction with us."

"Not having a father as a guide affected my perception of men and my standards. I felt unwanted and that my growth and emotional stability weren't worthy of my dad's investment. I felt discarded and lonely. I didn't have a man to provide valuable feedback, help me sort things out, or correct my thinking errors. I didn't have a daddy as a lighthouse to guide my way to adulthood. I wanted discipline; many times, I felt out of control. I ached to be hugged and kissed by my daddy."

"Some people told me I was cute- but I didn't feel attractive. I only dated men uglier than me so that I would feel pretty. When an attractive boy asked me for a date, I said no. I didn't feel worthy of him. How could I be appealing to a nice-looking guy when I felt so ugly? I used alcohol and weed to drug myself and convince me that right was wrong. When my maternal grandfather died, my bad behavior escalated. He was the only father figure I ever had. I started dating at 12 and experimenting with sex. I wanted to feel something other than numb. I partied and got drunk a lot. I did whatever I wanted. I was furious. I cursed teachers, and I jumped in my mamas' face using disrespectful language. I acted out frequently. I was uncontrollable. I sneaked boys into the house and stole from stores. One mall banished me from shopping there ever again."

"At school, a bunch of girls attacked me. Fear, nervousness, and depression became more prominent in my life. I asked my dad to take my sister and me. He said, "No. I don't want you.""

Alice's' sense of rejection is profound and evident from her statements. According to Robert Rannigan, Are You A Distant Dad? goodmanproject.com., when there is "lack of paternal attention, children are more likely to act out or misbehave. The psychologically distant father can increase the risk of destructive activities like smoking, poor social skills, or, crime." Information posted by The Fatherless Generation says, "85% of children who exhibit behavioral disorders come from fatherless homes." (Center for Disease Control).

"When I think about my dad, I feel regret for the interaction we never had. I used to hate him as a teenager but I don't anymore. I am still afraid of rejection by men. It would reignite the pain I felt when my father said he didn't want me.

I believe my dad's rejection causes the thirsty behaviors I've exhibited in relationships. I've been too clingy, had persistent thoughts about the person, stalked, behaved in embarrassing ways, been upset more than happy in the relationship, felt lonely, had sex when I didn't want to, tolerated cheating and remained in bondage. I tried to control my partner's behavior and even gave him money. In the beginning of the relationship I felt agonizing loneliness when we weren't together. I endured being slapped and punched. I got pregnant at 16. After I had three kids, one man asked who would want you with those kids? I echoed his question and repeated it to myself."

Dads4Kids Fact Sheet, Bill Muehlenberg, August 2014, reports "a US study found that girls who grow up without a father are 111% more likely to have children as teenagers."

"Now that I'm older I've learned about my father's history. His dad wasn't an active part of his life. As a child his discipline often consisted of being beaten with a belt while naked. Sometimes he was awakened and told to strip before the beating. Other times the attack occurred after a bath while he was wet."

This father's childhood experiences may explain, in part, his inability to connect with his children. A person abused in childhood learns ways of tamping down emotions to cope with painful experiences. Ignoring childhood needs for safety and honor assures that they won't occur. It appears that Alice's' dad learned to survive life's pain by using alcohol-induced escape. The saying 'hurt people hurt people' is apropos. Sometimes psychological distress is so absorbing people are unaware of the hurt they are causing others.

Alice's answers to the questions on codependency are: "I put the needs of my children and my patients before mine. I overwork because I feel guilty. I have said yes when I wanted to say no. Feeling wanted is important to me. I worry a lot especially about the safety of my children. Generally, I am too passive in a relationship. I am comfortable with my boundaries. In my earlier life I participated in four or five unhealthy relationships. As a teenager and young adult, the desires of guys were more important. I am good at knowing what other people are doing wrong and I don't hesitate to tell them."

Alice discovered that her rejection wounds cannot heal if she nurses them. Admittedly she didn't receive the support and affirmation she craved as a child but she can parent herself. She can provide the love and self-care missing from her early years. Self-management is an inside job which starts when thinking is changed. The adage as a person thinks in the heart, so is he or she is correct. At the age of 22, Alice told a friend, "I am tired of the way I've been living; I need Jesus." Her friend agreed to attend church with her. When Alice's soul melted with heaviness, she chose to gain strength from God's Word and to permit Jesus to be her burden bearer. Alice's attitude and behavior has changed because she is using a different rulebook. If Alice is committed to raising psychologically healthy children, she can give them what she did not have.

If Alice was co-dependent at one time, she isn't any longer. She made a conscious choice to stop the pattern of self-destructive actions.

Alice provides care for hospice patients as a certified nurse assistant (CNA). Her long- term goal is to earn a Bachelor of Science in Nursing (BSN) after her children leave the nest.

Action Steps

What are your primary self-care needs?

_____

_____

_____

_____

_____

List the ways you will nurture yourself.

_____

_____

_____

_____

_____

What do you admire the most about yourself?

_____

_____

_____

_____

_____

Cheryl Burton

What will you do to develop yourself?

_____

_____

_____

_____

_____

What are the necessary qualities of your ideal husband?

_____

_____

_____

_____

_____

Discuss your thoughts about forgiving your dad.

_____

_____

_____

_____

_____

How will you control the negative thinking that says you're worthless?

_____

_____

_____

_____

_____

Are you willing to implement the necessary steps to reconnect with your father? What strategy will you use?

_____

_____

_____

_____

_____

Chapter 12
Violent Dad: Holly' Story

---

*"Daughters exposed to a violent father select
a violent mate"*

Cheryl Burton

Holly recalls that at nine-years-old her stepfather became a part of her family. She said "my mom married him because he had a lovely house in a quiet neighborhood. Mom wanted my eight-year-old sister and me to be safe instead we met a violent and jealous man. It began when my stepfather showed up at my mom's job unexpectedly. Mom worked in a dry-cleaners near our elementary school. My sister and I would meet her and travel home together after mom closed-up. If my mom was talking to a male customer when my stepdad came, his eyes narrowed and he stood close to them to listen. When we got home, stepdad grasped mom by the throat and yelled, 'you whore.' It seemed wherever we went -to the store or my grandmother's house my stepdad showed up. My mom told me that at a dance my stepdad gripped her arm and said," go home." Eventually mom became fed up and we escaped one night while he slept. We had to walk to a bus stop because mom didn't have a car. A block from the house we saw my stepdad following us in his orange Chevy. My mom shouted run! I was terrified as we ran through an alley. Stepdad caught us and said,' get in the car.' Back at home he grabbed mom's throat. We could hear him cursing and my mom begging. My sister and I stayed in our beds frightened and crying. I feel ashamed we didn't try to help our mother. We were scared he might hit us. The next day my mom called her mother to pick us up. My grandmother took us to my uncle's house and my mom quit her job. But it wasn't over. My stepdad stalked mom. One- day he found her and put a gun in her back and whispered, 'don't scream.' A nearby man asked, 'Is he bothering you?' Mom shook her head; no. Mom was afraid stepdad would shoot. As stepdad left, he said, 'you can't get away from me.' One day the stalking stopped. Stepdad entered a hospital with a nervous breakdown after his mother's stabbing death during a home invasion. We never saw him again."

"When I was thirteen my mom remarried my dad, who had been in prison. Instead of life becoming better it got worse. Daddy was a heroin addict. He sold our new clothes, stereo, TV's and even the washing machine for a 'fix.' His drug addict friends hung around our house. I didn't feel safe around them. When mom came home from work, she told the druggies to get out."

"I didn't like being at home so I spent most days with friends. I started smoking cigarettes and drinking at thirteen. I stopped smoking for a short time when mom discovered me stealing her cigarettes. Instead of attending school I hung out. I had never been a good student.

I was ashamed that I repeated Kindergarten because I wouldn't talk and even worse my sister and I ended up in the same grade. I didn't speak because I missed my sister who was 11 months younger.

Besides I had never interacted with boys; they were scary. I sucked my thumb several years for comfort. I believed I was my sister's protector. When a boy at school bullied her, I beat him up. By spending so much time in the streets I learned to fight."

"My most unpleasant memory of my father was when he hit me in the face with his fist after I screamed, I hate you! We argued because he insisted, I clean up after my dogs. I love dogs but don't like cleaning up after them. Plus, I had zero respect for my drug-addicted father who stole the family's TV and clothes. He didn't have the right to tell me what to do. The heroin made him act crazy. I saw him crawling down the hall with a lighter looking for whatever."

"Dating and sexual experiences began at fifteen. My first date was handsome and a smooth talker. We had a fling without commitment or confusion. He may have been my first son's father. I'm not sure since I had sex with a couple of guys. At fifteen I received a beautiful engagement ring from a 6'5", nice-looking, charming, sweet man. I was 5'6" and attracted to taller men, the taller the better. We planned to marry when he completed military service. When he drank, he would slap my face or punch my body. He was always sorry later. I stayed with him because he was kind most of the time."

"I cheated on my fiancé; I was lonely. I met a 6'7" man who received a purple heart for bravery. His purple heart, height and writeup in a local paper impressed me. He was a sharp dresser but unattractive. I didn't want to have a baby by him; besides I already had a son. Ex-military man was available and I wanted company. My fiancé sent monthly checks for me to save. Military man convinced me to use two payments for his ex-girlfriend's abortion. He stole my engagement ring and gave it to another woman who pawned it. When my fiancé heard I cheated, lost the ring and gave away two checks he dumped me."

"When military man drank or was angry, he was violent and hit me. I was young, gullible and naive. I married my abuser anyway. Military man said he was sorry after beating me up and promised he wouldn't do it again. He was a cheater. When he got mad at his woman in the street, he beat me. We were married for two years. I left him when he put his knee on my toddler sons' chest and hit him. His action caused me to attack him to get him away from my boy. He beat me up instead."

"I met another 6'6" man who later became my husband. He was kind to my son and frightened all other men away. Military man attempted to reconnect but my future husband threatened his life. To retaliate military man called the fire department and said our house was burning."

"My new husband had a good job and liked to get high; so, did I. His main drawback was jealousy and violence. He didn't want me hanging out in clubs. I stopped the night he stalked me and brought my son into the nightclub. I felt humiliated."

Once he hung me upside down over a second-floor outside balcony and threatened to drop me if I continued clubbing. When I kept sneaking out the house, he slapped my face and blackened both eyes. I settled down after the birth of our second son. My husband and I loved to travel. We took annual family vacations touring the U.S. which calmed my desire to party."

"Although my husband was a wife beater, I forgave him. He didn't receive good teachings as a child. His father killed his mother when my husband was five. His dad went to prison and my husband went to foster care. When he was a teenager my husband lived with his paternal grandmother. My husband needed to be certain I loved him, that is the reason he wanted to control me."

"My husband and I both had bad childhoods. I never felt protected or received affection from my parents. My happiness came from drinking and being high. A sad memory was my mom didn't come to my high school graduation. Mom didn't get my cap and gown or high school ring. I was the only student who wore a suit. I cried on the way home by bus from the ceremony. It hurt that I didn't go to prom. My husband and I didn't have a father who was supportive, considerate, loving and our back-up. My husband provided those characteristics for our family. I became the loving mother he didn't have in childhood."

"My marriage lasted forty years. The last ten years were painful. My husband developed heart failure from smoking, drinking and 60 extra pounds. I retired early to take care of him. He didn't qualify for surgery unless he lost weight and stopped smoking and drinking. But he wouldn't follow the doctor's advice. When he died, I lost my 'boo' and my foundation. My husband helped me feel safe. Life was never the same again."

Was Holly co-dependent? See for yourself. Holly says," I used to put other people's needs first because I considered myself helping them. I don't do it now. All of my relationships were unhealthy except my last marriage. The unhealthy relationships had arguing, confusion and disagreements. Most of the time I'm too passive and people use me. When I get angry, I change to very aggressive by being loud, yelling and cussing. Then I feel bad because I hurt the person's feelings. I don't care too much about other people's values or judgments, I don't want to hurt their feelings. I don't overdo or work too hard. I have weak boundaries. I don't want to be lied about or see other people mistreated or used. I need to control things in my life not necessarily control others. I enjoy being needed and am happy to help others. I have learned not to worry a lot. Worry and stress causes my Chron's (inflammatory bowel) disease to flare up. I am good at knowing what other people are doing wrong in their life. When I was younger, 75% of the time I said yes when I wanted to say no; now it's 5% of the time."

Holly's responses suggest she tended toward co-dependency when she was younger. She still gravitates toward people-pleasing evidenced by her statement, "I don't want to hurt the person's feelings."

Sometimes speaking your beliefs even without malice will cause other people to feel hurt. Each person is responsible for their feelings. People pleasers and codependents tend to elevate other people's desires above theirs. Therapist Ann Stoneson says," people pleasers are preoccupied with what others think and feel. They are also fearful of seeming mean. Kids who grew up in a troubled home allow others to take advantage of them."

Holly said," when I was young, I was thirsty. I had to have a man in my life. (Needing a man in your life is also a sign of co-dependency). Men were easy to get in the bars and clubs. I didn't stalk anyone they chased me. I tolerated cheating, physical and verbal abuse from boyfriends and husbands. My second husband was abusive but he didn't cheat. Violence was the only way he knew to get me to stop going out. I made excuses for each man's lousy treatment. I don't think the physical abuse of my mother impacted my choice of men."

Several researchers disagree with Holly about the impact of witnessed violence on children. As we've learned from other stories people gravitate toward the familiar. "When children witness violence, they are more likely to be abused as adults" according to domesticshelter.org. 2014. These same children "experience poor self-esteem."

Lois M. Collins, Deseret.com says, "the best predictor of whether you will be in a violent relationship is whether you grew up in one." Relationship specialists write that violence begets violence. Being exposed to violent interactions as a child portend higher risk for experiencing violence in adolescent and adult relationships. Another conclusion is a "daughter may be more susceptible to alcoholism, drug use, promiscuity and domestic violence. A writer for women'shealth.gov. says," children who have experienced domestic violence are at higher risk for repeating the cycle or entering into an abusive relationship. A child who witnessed domestic abuse has low self-esteem."

Holly has offered a clue of poor self-esteem although she didn't say it directly. Holly drank alcohol and smoked cigarettes and marijuana for 57 years. Those chemicals helped her escape life's harsh realities. She was addicted to her crutches like her father was addicted to his- like father, like daughter. According to respected resources like the American Heart Association, "nicotine (in cigarettes) is as addictive as heroin and cocaine."

Holly didn't receive praise, affection or direction from her parents. Her father had drug problems and her mother repeatedly chose poor male influencers who detracted from the family's safety and security. Holly's mom may have been distracted from fulfilling her daughter's needs because of the overwhelm in her life. Holly was like a ship without an anchor. Holly admitted being afraid when she heard or saw her mom's abuse.

In childhood boundaries were absent. Holly didn't have a curfew and she wasn't required to be at home. In adulthood Holly didn't set personal boundaries that informed others of acceptable and unacceptable behaviors. Holly didn't insist that her boyfriend's treat her with respect.

Self-confident girls and women demand respectful treatment of their body and emotions. Holly excused or tolerated psychological abuse. A girl or woman with poor self-worth expects people to maltreat her.

Another sign of Holly's diminished self-value was her focus on repeating Kindergarten. She fixated on the shame of repeating a grade as evidence of not being smart. Holly said, "you have to be stupid to fail Kindergarten."

Holly sounded sad when she recalled the events surrounding her high school graduation. As an adult she understands the reasons her mom didn't provide what she needed. But, Holly said, "I still suffered. As a teenager I believed I didn't matter."

Holly attended a six-week training to work at a major company. She spent 40 years at that job. She advanced from an entry-level position to a supervisor in customer service. Holly said, "The company never suspended me. I felt important because I helped customers. My dream was to be a highway patrol woman or an 18-wheeler semi-truck driver. My second husband said no to both choices. He said I was too emotional to be an officer and too vulnerable for the truck stop crowd."

Action Steps

Complete these statements.

I deserved abuse because:

_____

_____

_____

_____

I feel obligated to take care of people in need because:

_____

_____

_____

_____

What value do you receive from providing care for others?

_____

_____

_____

_____

What rejection, neglect or abandonment causes fear of one of them occurring again?

_____

_____

_____

_____

_____

How did witnessing your mothers' abuse impact your choice of male partners?

_____

_____

_____

_____

How did your partners behave when upset?
Do you notice any similarities?

_____

_____

_____

_____

_____

List the qualities that help you excel as a customer service representative and supervisor?

_____

_____

_____

_____

_____

What are the reasons your parents couldn't meet your childhood needs?

_____

_____

_____

_____

Have you forgiven your parents for their poor care? Explain.

_____

_____

_____

_____

_____

Chapter 13
Sexual Abuser Dad: Brookes' Story

"A violated body creates a wounded soul"

Cheryl Burton

Imagine what it is like to be ten-years-old and chased by fear. Brookes' nightmare began when her mother changed to the night shift and Brooke and her stepfather were alone in the house. Brooke said," I was asleep when he got in bed with me. I awakened to him feeling my body. I screamed and he laughed and said, 'there's no one to help you, be still.' The first time he rubbed all over my body while I lay there afraid. When he got up, he said, "If you tell your mother I will hurt you." I cried myself to sleep and I didn't tell. I asked my mom for a lock on my door but I couldn't say the real reason. I told her I wanted to feel safe. My mom smiled and said, 'you are safe. Your stepdad will protect you.' I asked mom for a dog but she said 'no, I don't want to take care of a pet.'

Brooke said, "whenever my mom worked nights, I pushed my dresser against my bedroom door. I had trouble sleeping and nightmares of my stepdad attacking me. Several days passed then one night I awoke to him in bed with me. He put his hand over my mouth and raped me. When it was over, he told me to clean up, change the sheets and wash them. He continued to abuse me until he and mom divorced. I kept silent until I was thirty-five. By then I was living in another state and was a single parent of two sons. When I told my mom, at first, she didn't believe me. Then she asked, 'why didn't you tell me before and why now?' When I told her, I didn't want to hurt her and of his threats she held me and we both cried."

It isn't uncommon that disclosure hibernates for several years before the reveal. According to mosac.net (mothers of sexually abused children), "28% of sexual abuse survivors say they never told anyone about being raped during childhood. Of those who did tell 47% didn't talk about it until five years after the rape occurred." A sad effect is that the traumatic experience is "continuing to shape the developing child and adult she becomes" according to a psychologist who specializes in childhood sexual abuse.

Brooke told me her story while she braided my hair several years ago. She hadn't told her mom yet. I suggested she talk to her mom. My advice was before I studied counseling and sexual abuse and sexual addiction. I didn't know to suggest Brooke also get professional advice to help her face and overcome the damage.

Brooke moved to another state and I was unable to interview her for the book. Although the details are incomplete, her story is representative of trauma some girls endure and deserves exposure.

Brooke isn't alone. According to childhoodtauma.org., "one of three females experience sexual abuse before 18." As previously mentioned, more sexual abuse occurs at the hands of a family member or another supposedly trustworthy adult.

The American Psychological Association (APA) defines sexual abuse as "unwanted sexual activity." Abuse victims report the wrongdoer either touched, kissed or used objects to violate them sexually via their vagina, anus or mouth. Sometimes the victim is forced to stroke the penis or perform oral sex. Even babies are recruited for oral sex. Girls or women can violate too. The victim reports shock, disgust or denial. The APA writes that "sexual abuse may cause a person to become shy, withdrawn or to develop any number of mental disorders."

Sexual violation has enduring effects. According to addiction specialists who treat alcohol, drugs and eating disorders, 90% of their patients have a known history of some form of abuse. The National Institute of Drug Abuse concurs, and reports that "women who have suffered some form of sexual abuse during childhood are up to three times more likely to develop a substance abuse disorder." Some victims develop shopping, spending or eating disorders.

When I counseled ex-offenders in a reentry program a large percentage of both men and women reported sexual abuse experience; that's when I became interested in studying sexual abuse and sexual addiction. Many of the ex-offender counselees struggled with drug or alcohol addiction.

A victim of sexual abuse displays tell-tale signs. The following actions may signal molestation:

Reluctance to visit or spend time with a person.

Withdrawn behavior.

Inappropriate sexual knowledge by a young child.

Expression of shame or guilt.

Sexual promiscuity.

Substance abuse.

Depression or fear.

Self-loathing.

Difficulty trusting.

Self-mutilation e.g. cutting, or sticking self with pins or other sharp objects to relieve tension or anxiety.

Symptoms of Post-Traumatic Stress Disorder (PTSD). Possible triggers are environmental conditions similar to the time(s) of the abuse; smells, (one woman reported a skunk smell during rape) or specific sounds.

Nightmares.

Difficulty walking or sitting without pain.

Unexplained bloody clothing.

Poor self-esteem.

A significant change in eating habits involving loss of appetite or gorging on food.

It is vital to investigate the cause of the above signs before assuming abuse has occurred. My goal is to increase the awareness of the signs and prevalence of childhood sexual assault. Then adults can protect and advocate for at-risk youths.

Action Steps

If you have experienced sexual trauma seek help from a specialist in childhood sexual abuse. It won't be easy to deal with buried issues, but there is freedom on the other side of pain.

Journaling about the experience can be beneficial depending on your personality and ability to face the agony without assistance. Journaling permits the expression of anguish, fears and anger in relative safety. The downside is a reluctance to face the past authentically. The temptation is to continue to hide from the truth which keeps you stuck.

Some women write a blog as a resource for victims; by helping others they help themselves to be an effective overcomer.

Online groups with peer support are available in some areas.

Chapter 14
Non-Protector Dad: Tamar's Story

"You abandoned me when I needed you the most"

Cheryl Burton

Even though this story occurred in ancient Israel in 990 B.C., it is relevant for today's' women. According to Department of Justice statistics, 300,000 U.S. women experience rape every year. The Huff Post reports Center for Disease Control estimates of rape as high as 1.3 million U.S. women. If you think rape happens only to lower and middle- class women, you are wrong. It can occur in the highest places. Tamar's' story takes place in the King's palace.

Can Tamar's story validate the shame and humiliation you have felt as an assault victim left to self-soothe instead of protected by a caring father? Decide for yourself after reading my paraphrase of the story. Read the full account in 2: Samuel 13:12-13. (Bible).

Tamar was a privileged woman. She wore an expensive robe befitting the virgin daughter of royalty. She lived in protective custody on the palace grounds. The biblical account describes Tamar as beautiful with good moral character. Her father was the courageous King David, the man after God's own heart. David received the label 'after God's own heart' as a young man. He made lots of mistakes but he repented and acknowledged his wrongdoing and asked for God's forgiveness. As a youth David slew the 9'9" Goliath but as King he left his daughter to fend for herself after a violent rape by her half-brother, Amnon. Based on my research King David was a distant, uninvolved father as it relates to his daughter. David was angry when he learned of Tamar's rape but he neither comforted her or confronted Amnon. According to Dr. John MacArthur, King James Version (KJV) Study Bible," David abdicated his responsibility both as a king and a father." Tamar must have known what to expect from her father since after the rape she sought solace from her full brother Absalom.

The story begins with her half-brother Amnon telling his cousin Jonadab that he was sick with love for Tamar. What Amnon felt can better be titled lust. Together the two men hatched a plot to convince King David of Amnon's illness that could be treated by the hand-made cakes of Tamar. Note, David cared enough to visit Amnon's residence and ask about his health.

The King didn't know his first-born son, Amnon was a deceiver. It is easy to fool a father blind to his offspring's character. David responded to Amnon's request by sending a message to Tamar. Being an obedient daughter and accustomed to serving a man's wishes Tamar complied. She went to Amnon's chamber and prepared the cakes. When the food was ready, Amnon sent the servants from the room leaving he and Tamar alone. Then Amnon demanded that Tamar hand feed him. When Tamar neared him, Amnon, clutched her hand and said," lie with me, my sister."

Tamar protested and tried to reason with him. She said the act would be wicked, disgraceful, heap shame on her and cause him to be labeled a fool. It would tarnish his reputation when he became the next king.

Tamar told Amnon to ask David and he would agree to their marriage. Her words didn't extinguish his passion, he raped her.

After the heinous act Amnon told Tamar to get up and get out. Scripture says he hated her and felt disgust. The hatred he felt for her was more significant than the love he claimed he had. Tamar pleaded with Amnon saying, "No; indeed! This evil of sending me away is worse than the other you did to me." 2 Samuel 13:16 (KJV) Amnon told his servant to put this woman out and bolt the door behind her. He depersonalized Tamar during and after the rape by ignoring her feelings and not using her name. Lust doesn't care who it hurts. Once Amnon experienced her body, he wanted nothing else to do with her. That is one of the hallmarks of desire. You'll recognize it when the person doesn't want to spend time together after the sex.

After her banishment Tamar tore her robe, a sign of profound grief over her irreversible loss. She put ashes on her head and ran to Absalom's home weeping aloud. Tamar lost her virginity, an opportunity to marry and have children. According to biblical scholars, as an Israelite woman, "Tamar's situation was a living death." Rape isn't just violence against the body it is a blight on a person's soul.

Absalom said to Tamar, "has Amnon been with you?" After hearing her truth Absalom counseled her to be quiet; he would take care of the matter. It took two years for Absalom to exact revenge and kill Amnon. Amnon's inability to curb his ardor cost his life and lost him the role as the next King.

Absalom didn't remain unscathed. He ran away to avoid the charge of premeditated murder. The Bible said, David mourned for both sons, but failed to invite Absalom to return home. Absalom's resentment against David mushroomed. Absalom led a rebellion against David that cost Absalom's life. This sordid tale reveals the wages of uninvolved parenting. In David's case his payment was the loss of two sons and the rape of his daughter.

According to scripture, King David had a deep abiding relationship with God his whole life. But David faltered when he had the opportunity to display to his daughter the comfort and direction he had known with God. Tamar's half-brother Amnon violated the law that stated "you shall not uncover the nakedness of your sister."

Leviticus 18:11. Tamar bore the stigma from each man's failings for the rest of her life.

Today's woman needs to stay aware of the prevalence of acquaintance rape. According to the Illinois Coalition Against Sexual Assault (CASA)[*] acquaintance rape:

Can occur any time, any place.

The rapist can be a date, neighbor, boss, colleague, delivery person, repair worker or someone else you know.

A woman is four times more likely to be raped by an acquaintance than a stranger.

The typical age of victims is 15-24. (An intruder raped my sixtyish-year-old grandmother in her home by climbing up a second-floor balcony and breaking the lock on her kitchen door.)

One in four college women were victims of rape or attempted rape when they were a student. Eighty-four percent of them knew the rapist. Fifty-seven percent of the crimes happened during a date. (Dr. Mary Koss-researcher at Kent State University)

Twelve percent of college men reported that they had physically restrained a woman to gain sexual advantage.

---

[*] Permission granted from ICASA for use.

Chapter 15
Disappointment Dad: My Story

Sometimes a daughter's love for her dad changes to hatred the more time they spend together. That doesn't mean she doesn't still yearn for a father's love and support; it simply means she has learned not to count on her dad to fulfill her needs. I read this poignant tag line on a post titled an open letter to my dad- "You are the first man to break my heart." I could have written that tag.

My earliest daddy memory occurred at eight -years old. Our relationship must have been pleasant before that because I called him the affectionate term Daddy-man. I don't remember the excuse my mom gave me for dad not being a part of the family, I only remember writing him letters telling how much I missed him and desperately wanted him to return. He'd answer my messages and assure me he missed me too. I fantasized about the pleasure we'd share when he returned.

When my father came home, I was thrilled to see him. My feelings rapidly began to change. He wasn't anything like my fairy tale version of him. I wanted a father like Robert Young in the sitcom Father Knows Best. Robert Young was thoughtful, kind interactive and involved with his family. He participated in solving their problems and soothing their hurts within thirty minutes. He was hardworking, intelligent and affectionate. My father was a liar, cheat and heroin addict. He rarely worked. He stole our TV's, stereo system, washing machine and clothing to support his habit. He exposed me to his drug-addict associates. Only one of the men misbehaved toward me. He asked if I would be his mistress. At thirteen, I didn't understand the word, I had to consult the dictionary. I didn't mention his offer to either parent. One advantage to my exposure to the drug culture was I didn't want to become a member of their community nor did I want a mate who used drugs. I later learned in real-life Robert Young suffered with depression and a biochemical imbalance he medicated with alcohol. He was a human being with human struggles. Young received treatment for his problem and eventually my father did too. My father lost his family and their respect because of his actions.

I started working at nine-years-old to earn extra money. I babysat for a neighbor and cleaned another neighbors home. At fifteen, I worked from 6:30 a.m.-3:00 p.m. in a hospital cafeteria on the weekends. At 5:30 a.m. I walked three blocks to catch the first bus. I huddled in a doorway until it arrived. Fortunately, no one ever assaulted me. The second bus-stop had Forest Park as the background. Without daylight it was dark and scary. In the winter, I felt cold and lonely but no one ever bothered me. I took left-over sandwiches and salads home from the cafeteria to ensure our family dinner. It was during this time the resentment against my dad grew. I experienced the uncomfortable poisonousness of hatred. Before I entered our house after work, I looked through the front porch picture window. I examined the living room and adjacent bedroom for missing items. The stereo and TV were like a yo-yo, here today and gone to the pawnshop tomorrow.

I never knew my dad as a person. We never talked about his hopes and dreams and mine. I don't recall us engaging in fun activities or spending time together except when he watched military movies. The two facts I know are my dad liked to clean the house. He also enjoyed cooking a southern-style breakfast of fried chicken, mashed potatoes and home-made biscuits. His mother was a domestic and cook, he learned his skills from her. Although, I grieve not having my dream-daddy, I appreciate that my dad wasn't sexually or physically abusive. He abused himself more than he did others. I don't know the reason my dad chose his lifestyle; my mom says my dad's father was an honorable man. Perhaps my dad started using drugs to evade memories of the horror of military service.

I developed an insatiable thirst for a person to fill the hole in my soul. I had an unspoken question for the males I dated- 'are you the one'? They didn't know they were competing with a fantasy man culled from my dreams and the enmeshed fairy tales in my psyche. As a child, I read every fairy-tale story available at the public library. They always ended with 'and they lived happily ever after.' I sought the bliss of the happy ever after. Heck, I didn't know, until recently that my experiences sowed the seeds of codependency.

At thirteen, I met a sixteen-year-old who dominated thirteen years of my life. He was' drop-dead gorgeous', fun-loving, generous and persistent. He wanted to marry me. I wouldn't have sex with him and I know that's what drove his urgency for marriage. I promised myself, I wouldn't have to tell my mother I was pregnant without being married.

Many of my schoolmates desired to have him because he looked good. I was insecure about my looks; I felt too tall and not physically appealing. When my future husband zeroed in on me my self-esteem improved. I didn't have the maturity to look beneath his physical appeal to his character. Over time I learned a person can look good on the outside and be rotten to the core. I wished I had used my Father Knows Best template as a checkoff.

We were teenagers, with the idealism of youth. He was my imaginary knight-in-shining-armor. I was his princess. We were adventurous and loved similar activities like stargazing, canoeing, horseback riding, picnics and making creative sandwiches. We loved hugging and cuddling which satisfied my desire for physical closeness and touch. He pressured me for sex but I was steadfast in saying no. We spent available time together. When our concerned mothers attempted to nix our relationship, we became more determined to be together. Neither of us had a dad in the home.

My first husband's not entirely to blame. I was weak. At eighteen I married him despite my misgivings. He was twenty-one. We didn't have a life plan. I told myself, things would work out. I lied to myself. I learned firsthand the truth of the statement, 'what does light have to do with darkness?' I wanted to become a social worker, or a teacher, he didn't have any expressed professional desires. He worked as a gas station attendant and in other menial jobs during the eight years we were married. He graduated from marijuana to heroin. He assured me if I used heroin, I wouldn't become addicted. That was the fib he told himself. I had minuscule respect for him and was verbally abusive. I demeaned him for not being a man. I demanded that he attend truck-driving school and although I dropped him off at class, he never completed training. Another woman picked him up. Now that my understanding has improved, I think he had an undiagnosed learning disability. He was a life-long cheater. Plus, he tried to sabotage my efforts at self-improvement.

After eight years of drama, lying, cheating, heroin use and stealing I divorced him. The final straw occurred when my husband sold the unique, wooden rocking chair, the heart-shaped diamond necklace and smaller appliances I valued for drugs. I hated him and didn't want him in my vicinity. I had attracted and married my dad. I left every remaining item we had accumulated during our union and moved to Chicago, Illinois but through stealth he found me. My ex-husband was 'hoovering', attempting to suck me back into his clutches. He left me alone after a muscular Chicago policeman, fifty-pounds heavier and a few inches taller, threatened to beat and arrest him.

I'm a slow learner. I was still looking for love in all the wrong places and searching for love in too many faces. In Chicago, I looked for and found my next husband while volunteering at the USO, (United States Organization). He came to my desk with a charming smile and sparkling eyes. We chatted, flirted and left together. We grabbed a bite to eat and spent a few hours viewing lake Michigan. It was a romantic interlude. We talked half the night learning what the other person chose to share. We married a few months later. He was a decent guy, pleasant, and willing to work. I was impressed by his physique, that like me, he loved poetry and had served as a marine. But he had significant unresolved 'mommy issues' that mirrored my 'daddy issues.' Our baggage became a burden that strangled the union. I married him too soon after my first marriage ended. I hadn't done the necessary healing or understanding of the reasons I made a colossal mistake with my first marriage. I was bored, thirsty and restless, still searching for 'the one.'

While working as a respiratory therapy program coordinator, mistake number three appeared. He was charming like a snake. He invited me to dinner and I accepted. He told me his philosophy of life but I disregarded his message. I cheated with a man who recognized my vulnerability. I hurt my husband when I divorced him. I traded my husband for another liar, cheater and deceiver disguised as carefree, fun-loving and adventurous. I've learned if you don't learn a life lesson you repeat it until you do.

Man, number three waved little red flags demonstrating his lack of good character, but I chose to overlook them. I desired the fun and excitement he offered. We both wanted to start anew in San Francisco, California. We were respiratory therapists and jobs were easy to find. We packed our clothes and spent two weeks touring the country on our way to San Fran. The Rocky Mountains, Estes Park, Colorado, Colorado Springs, Mount Rushmore, and the Painted desert delighted our eyes. I noticed my companion had sticky fingers and stole small items at a few gift shops. But I didn't say anything because I didn't want to be alone, so I was complicit. My cohort branched into taking from me.

I discovered he was very prideful with a sense of entitlement. He said his mother warned him about the folly of pride. He responded, "if I don't have my pride, I don't have anything." While still in Chicago he left his roommate holding the bag for his share of the back rent. But I overlooked that flag too.

How could I complain when he didn't pay me back the thousand - dollar loan I secured for him? He had demonstrated his untrustworthiness. My daddy said," if you see a fool, bump his head." I needed my head hit to wake up to the truth of his lack of character and mine.

San Francisco was too chilly for me. We moved to Los Angeles and shared a loft apartment for three years. Number three was a prolific cheater; I was an infrequent one. When I became weary of the relationship, I moved home to Saint Louis, Missouri. My hungry eyes continued to search for 'the one.'

After two short term involvements, I married my current husband. We have been married for thirty-six years and have two adult sons.

Marriage didn't satisfy my soul hunger. I had to learn the message from St. Augustine, "Lord, you have made us for yourself. Our hearts are restless until we have found our rest in Thee." I was still searching for the 'one'. I kept thinking; I must find someone to fulfill this need. Be careful of what you wish for, you just might get it. I met my 'soul-mate' at work. We began as friends, who connected when we weren't busy. One night after our chat time, I felt shock as I realized, I was in love with him. But the reality is I needed him to mitigate my unhappiness.

We occasionally went to breakfast after our nightshift ended. Then we began spending hours together seeing a movie, going to Faust Sculpture park, the Botanical Garden, the Planetarium and other fun activities. We enjoyed talking, or sharing a meal. He delighted me with his magic tricks. He was a good listener and mentor. For the first time in my life I felt loved. He was like a daddy. We spent three meaningful years together.

Officially we were friends but I developed a soul-tie with my heart in bondage to him. In theory, a soul-tie results from a sexual relationship; that wasn't the case for me. We never had sex. However, he lived inside my head. Obsessive thoughts about him tracked me. I felt his presence everywhere. He was my escape hatch from life's problems. I felt anxious when I wasn't with him and comforted when I was. Then why was I more miserable than I'd ever been? Unbidden tears surfaced at the grocery store, in a movie, at work, while driving or preparing dinner. It was because I defied God's promptings to end this ungodly connection.

My soul mate and I were Christians. We discussed our commitment never to cause a person to stumble or sin because of our actions. My friend said, "you are incredibly needy, someone is going to hurt you." As my friend witnessed my struggle, he ended all contact. He said he couldn't manage both his pain and mine. He was dealing with deliberately untreated skin cancer and sky-high glucose levels from unmanaged diabetes, He desired the solitude of death to escape life's sorrows. I grappled with the pain of his loss for two years. Then, clarity arrived. God wanted my hope, adoration and commitment to reside in Him instead of another human being. During that period, I learned obedience to God by what I suffered. I am finally free of the soul tie and daddy issues. Jesus Christ answered my question, "are you the one" with I AM.

Before his death my father apologized for his wrongdoings. He had the pleasure of meeting his grandchild, my oldest son. I have forgiven my dad. I am sorry we never knew each other.

My story indicates I was codependent and thirsty. I spent many years as a people pleaser so people would like me. I believed people-pleasing made me worthy. It was compensation for me not loving myself. My poor self-esteem was at the root of my bad choices in men leading to unhealthy involvements. Even after I recognized corrupt behaviors in my partner, I stayed with him. A symbol of codependency is always wanting a significant person in your life. I had weak character with my only standard being that a man be physically and emotionally satisfying. How pitiful is that? I was suggestible and gullible to persuasion. I accepted lies because I first lied to myself.

I have learned I was an empath with a commitment to relieving other people's pain. Plus, I was a rescuer, dedicated to helping people overcome life's challenges. I had to learn the better way of being a helper in problem-solving. User's loved me because I willingly gave and they unabashedly took.

Improved self-awareness sensitized me to the magnitude of my negative self-talk. Self-recrimination was a constant companion I had to master and eliminate.

My marriage has become better as I have grown in self-understanding. I desire to be the Alpha in all relationships; I am learning to relinquish my desire to control others. My husband and I still butt heads because he is a first-born Alpha male and I am an Alpha female. He has proven worthy of my respect so I am occasionally submissive to his will. Learning to be submissive is a dynamic process. I think I know what others are doing wrong in their life. It is easier to be objective when your view isn't clouded with emotion or personal involvement. My challenge is to be discerning and not judgmental. I enjoy being needed by some people but I don't think I have a pathological desire. I don't want to be involved with any energy drainers.

Even though my childhood and adolescence were not ideal they didn't prevent me from achieving some of my goals. I knew I wanted a career in which I provided value to others. At seventeen, I enrolled in Harris Stowe Teachers College for a BA in Education. I heard about a new program; Inhalation Therapy that helped people manage their lung disease. I switched careers and at nineteen became registered as the first black Inhalation therapist in St. Louis, MO. The name inhalation changed to respiratory. I fulfilled my desire to teach by educating about respiratory principles at Forest Park Community College in St. Louis, MO., Malcolm X Community College in Chicago, Ill. and a proprietary college in LA., California.

While I was living in LA, California, I started a self-growth plan. I devoured self-improvement books. After returning to St. Louis I certified as a Christian counselor and in sexual addiction/sexual abuse. I earned a Masters in Rehabilitation counseling from Maryville University, St. Louis, MO. I studied with John Maxwell and earned certification as a coach specializing in self-leadership. Under the tutelage of Lisa Nichols, I have learned transformational coaching. My coaching business is Leading in Success, LLC. I have parlayed my love of writing and research into three books; Mastering the Art of Self-Leadership, Stories and Strategies; Stop Limiting Your Success and this current book. I believe it doesn't matter where you start, it matters where you end.

Chapter 16
12 Codependent Questions for Women

(Used with permission)

by Cherilynn Veland | Sep 4, 2013 | Relationships

Could you be codependent and not know it? Let's see.

Ask yourself:

Do you tend to put others' needs in front of yours?

Have you ever gotten into relationships that are unhealthy?

Are you sometimes too passive or too aggressive in your relationships?

Do you find yourself caring too much about others' opinions and judgments?

Do you tend to overdo or work too hard?

Do you either not have good enough boundaries or keep them so tight you can be rigid?

Do you feel the need to control things or others?

Do you enjoy being needed?

Do you worry a lot?

Do you ever get confused about what your needs are? And then find yourself frustrated with others?

Are you good at knowing what people are doing wrong in their life?

Have you ever said "yes" when you wanted to say "no"?

Definition of Codependency:

"Codependency is whenever you put others' needs in front of your own and the results are self-destructive. The definition of codependent behaviors has involved from it just being about a relationship with an addict or alcoholic. Now, we therapists recognize that codependency includes many self-destructive behaviors. Some of these behaviors are covered by a desire to help, please, or caretake others. Along with codependency comes lotsa' control stuff too. In my work, I have seen multitudes of women walk around with depression, anxiety, low self -esteem, and troubled relationships. Much of it is caused by codependent behavior."

You can read more in Cherilynn Velands' book *Stop Giving It Away: How to Stop Self-Sacrificing and Start Claiming Your Space, Power, and Happiness*

Chapter 17
Interview Questions: Are you a thirsty woman?

Did you ever behave as a thirsty woman?

Have you been accused of being too clingy?

Have you had obsessive thoughts about the person? Explain.

Have you ever stalked him in any way including his social media pages?

Have you ever engaged in embarrassing activity with him or because of him?

Are you fearful of criticism or rejection by him?

Have you tolerated being more upset than happy in your relationship?

Have you performed undesirable sex acts to hold onto him?

Have you endured feeling lonely in the relationship?

Do you feel agonizingly empty when you aren't in his presence?

Have you accepted him cheating even though you wanted exclusivity?

Have you tried to control his behaviors? What did you do?

Have you withstood physical, emotional or psychological abuse and made excuses for his behaviors?

Part Two:
Choosing A Partner

When deciding on a potential mate there are vital considerations. Three of the most important are will he provide a stable foundation for you and your children? Do you demonstrate mutual respect for your individuality, sensitivity to each other's needs and encourage one another's emotional, psychological and spiritual growth? Have you developed a litmus test for a man before you present the key to your heart?

The following are toxic partners to avoid.

Chapter 18
The Narcissist

The Narcissist: An egotistical, self-focused person, recognizable by the mantra, 'it's me me, all about me.'

If you become involved with a true narcissist get prepared for a roller coaster ride. He is the man featured in romantic novels or Lifetime movies. You'll recognize him standing out from the crowd. His attire is compelling; his body language self-confident, charm oozes from his pores; as your eyes connect a thrill surges through your body. His smile, physical attractiveness, humor and intelligence seal the deal. This master enchanter has captured you, hook, line and sinker. During the initial attraction period he seems almost perfect. After several months of delight, you notice these disturbing signals.

He exaggerates his accomplishments.

He gets enraged if you suggest he isn't correct about an issue; rightfulness is part of his DNA.

He is disturbingly arrogant and self-righteous.

He is very critical and a fault finder.

He must be in control of every element of the relationship; where you go; what you do; what you wear; who your friends are.

Every situation in his life must be perfect.

He has aced the blame game.

He is disinterested in changing to improve your connection.

He doesn't apologize even when he is wrong.

He treats you like a trophy instead of a person with emotional and physical needs.

He can't relate to your feelings because he lacks empathy.

He dominates the conversation; you can't get a word in edgewise.

He is a reckless driver.

He relies on drugs and or alcohol for psychological support.

He needs you as a cheerleader to affirm his superiority.

He is a serial cheater and engages in risky sexual behavior.

He is emotionally distant.

He is a liar; his word is untrustworthy.

He may resort to gaslighting behaviors to confuse and create doubt in you.

He disrespects you by yelling and calling you unflattering names.

He must be the center of attention and requires a boatload of flattering approval.

He has trouble maintaining longstanding committed relationships.

This list is neither exhaustive or complete. It is an amalgamation of characteristics from varied sources and my life experience. Its purpose is to provide red flags for your consideration and to warn of potential disaster if you choose a narcissist for a loved one. Because of the narcissist lack of empathy, untrustworthiness, reduced ability to connect with others and emotional unavailability he is unlikely to make a good parent.

If your illusion is that you can change him after marriage perish the thought. Think about how difficult it is to change yourself when you desire to be different. The narcissist I have met didn't wish to change. They didn't see anything wrong with their actions. Research into narcissistic behavior confirms that a narcissist sees himself as perfect and the other person the problem. If you are dissatisfied with your union with a narcissist, I suggest professional counseling for guidance and additional insight to manage the situation.

Common lies from a narcissist:

You are nothing without me; you're too weak to be alone.

Look at yourself; Who else would want you?

I'm not lying; I swear this is the truth; You must believe me; I am not a liar.

I'm like this because of my horrible background.

I'm not involved with this person; he or she is a stalker.

No one cares for you like I do.

You'll never have our kind of love with anyone else.

Your family and friends want to mess up our relationship.

She means nothing to me; you're my Queen.

My ex-wife was a cheater and a toxic person.

I used to be a player but I'm not anymore.

You are the woman of my dreams.

I need this weekend alone to think (when he wants to spend time with someone else).

I'm sorry, I promise I'll change.

Life has kicked my butt; I need drugs or alcohol to cope.

You are a 'psycho'; your mind is warped.

It's all your fault.

You need help for your mental dysfunction.

People at work are jealous of my looks and accomplishments, that's the reason I get fired.

These are mistruths women have reported hearing from their narcissistic mate. The purpose of the lie is to undermine your self-confidence and diminish your self-esteem. Remember the narcissist is adept at blaming others to shift the focus from him and make you detestable.

"The difference between a cat and a lie-the cat only has nine lives."

Mark Twain

Chapter 19
The Sociopath

The Sociopath: aka. Antisocial personality disorder; A cunning, master manipulator who must win at all costs.

Have you witnessed a big cat, like a cougar or leopard stalk a victim? They stare intently at a group of animals to identify the most vulnerable and weakest. The sociopath, like the big cat camouflages his actions to conceal intent until it's too late to resist. According to Tonja Petrella, Sociopathic Tendencies, "a sociopath has a good idea of who you are before they even meet you. They may have sized you up from afar and even watched you to determine your habits, likes and dislikes."

If you have a history of childhood wounds from abuse or neglect; if you are hungry for interaction, have low self-esteem or self-worth, or easily dominated you are the perfect victim for his charms and maneuvers. He is highly intelligent, intoxicating, and charismatic. If you agree to sex, he is an incredible lover. When the two of you interact, he identifies your vulnerabilities by your words and behaviors. He appears intuitive by telling you what you need. He thrives on playing head games with you.

A woman married to a sociopath said when she looked into her husbands' eyes she saw 'balls of ice.'

Your first line of defense begins by believing he exists. According to Web MD. and Martha Stout, The Sociopath Next Door four percent of the population have Antisocial personality disorder. The disorder exists in one percent of women and three percent of men.

A moral compass is "an internalized set of values and objectives that guide a person concerning ethical behavior and decision making." www.dictionary.com. The sociopaths' compass points south and includes all things evil; stealing, lying, cheating, hatred and punishment. His conscience is poorly developed or non-existent. Don't be fooled, he may have honed his abilities to appear reasonable. He looks normal.

The Sociopath can only give false love. His kind of love makes you more pliable to manipulation.

These are additional red flags he waves:

He 'love bombs', and promises you a perfect future. His kindness and attention are excessive in the early stages and when he feels you pulling away. Be suspicious instead of flattered.

His stare is penetrating and stirs your soul and makes you feel desirable. (He is a predator sizing you up as prey)

He wants to know about every part of your life. (It helps him design an effective strategy to use you.)

His alleged affection is 'over the top.' He is incapable of genuine love. Listen to your gut; your intuition doesn't lie.

He is showers you with compliments and hypnotizing charm that doesn't feel right.

He wants you to commit to a relationship too soon. He may pressure you to marry, combine finances, or move in together very early.

He gets angry if you refuse to have sex and ignores your reasons.

His actions and words don't align.

He is infuriated when he isn't in control; winning is his top priority.

He demonstrates a reckless disregard for his safety and that of others.

He is irresponsible in managing his obligations like paying debts and work requirements.

He lacks empathy or remorse when he has hurt you or others.

He seems to get pleasure from inflicting injury.

He seeks your pity when he feels trapped.

He relies on drugs or alcohol to self-soothe.

He is impulsive and fails to plan.

He is irritable and aggressive when he doesn't get what he wants.

He is deceitful and full of justification for lying and cheating.

He refuses to conform to social norms, i.e. the accepted standards of behavior for your social group.

He lies and cheats so much he has created a pattern. Pointing it out or arguing with him about his habit can leave you frustrated; it may be time to leave him.

He has poor parenting skills and will ignore his offspring.

He has violent tendencies and may hit you when enraged.

His responses change according to whom is asking the question.

He doesn't let you see his living conditions. He comes to your house or takes you to a hotel.

His life revolves around the con game.

Therapy may not help the sociopath because he won't tell the truth. Silva Hayes, In Love with a Sociopath says "he may feel more empowered since he is fooling a professional, feeding them a warped description of his life events and enjoying the therapists' full attention."

This list is from the Mayo Clinic writers; In Love with a Sociopath, Silva Hayes, 2015; Diagnostic and Statistical Manual of Mental Disorders (DSM-5); The Sociopath Next Door, Martha Stout; Sociopathic Tendencies, Tonja Petrella, Hub Pages, 2019.

Common Lies spoken by the Sociopath:

I will never lie or cheat.

I love you too much to hurt you.

I loved you the first time I saw you.

We share similar beliefs and dreams.

He promises undying commitment to win your affection.

You are the woman I've wanted all my life.

Your family or friends are using you.

The business wouldn't be successful without my superior knowledge.

I need you to invest in me to help launch our business.

He accompanies his denial with crocodile tears. (insincere expressions of sorrow)

I have trouble being honest because others have deceived me.

I am too talented to settle for just any job.

I thought you wouldn't love me if you knew about my massive debt or low credit score.

She threw herself at me and I couldn't resist.

I am trustworthy.

I can't get you pregnant.

What you believe isn't true.

Everyone thinks you're crazy; The sociopath tells your friends, family and colleagues you're mentally unbalanced.

My phone died or I was out of range of a cell tower.

I'll pay you back the money I owe.

Some of the listed lies come from personal experience; others from Donna Andersons' post on LoveFraud.com; 7 Classic Lies from a Sociopath.

Chapter 20
Commitment-phobe

A commitment-phobe says no to a binding relationship like marriage.

The commitment-phobe is the man to avoid if your goal is a long-term obligation like marriage. An honest man will reveal his intention in the beginning. One man told me he only wanted someone to spend time with and share pleasurable activities. Another man denied commitment- phobia; he pointed to a previous long - term relationship lasting more than a decade. He forgot an earlier statement admitting his fear of the legal consequences of marriage dissolution. He's not the only man with apprehensions regarding divorce. Divorce concerns determined in a study conducted by Rutgers University Marriage Project are the loss of half their pension, a portion of their savings and a share of property acquired during marriage. Some men believe a spouse would nix friendships and social activities they treasure. Others fear loss of control of their children or a wife will gain weight or become a tyrant.

Other men have made statements like; "I want to keep things light" or "I only want a casual relationship." If you think by playing the role of a wife, i.e. cooking, cleaning, and sex you can change his mind you may be inviting disappointment. Have you heard the saying, 'Why buy the cow when you can get the milk for free?'

You should also know that some men marry and yet remain uncommitted. These men are afraid or incapable of loving. A resource that may offer clarity is *Men Who Can't Love, How to*

Cheryl Burton

Recognize a Commitment Phobic Man Before He Breaks Your Heart, Steven Carter& Julia Sokol.

The man who chooses not to reveal this fear of dedicating himself to you may display these sure signs:

He has had a series of short-term relationships. One man admitted, "I've been with many, many women."

He never talks about a future with you.

He is over forty and has never been married. If he has, it was short-lived.

He avoids meeting your friends or family.

He doesn't introduce you to his peers or family.

He doesn't define your relationship. Notice the way he introduces you to other people; does he call you a girlfriend or a friend, or does he just say your name?

He is often unavailable via phone or texts.

He tells you he can't be in a serious relationship because he needs to work on himself.

He tells you he wants to keep things slow.

You must take the lead in planning together time.

He disappears and is unreachable for weeks.

He says, "I don't want to rush into anything."

He is secretive about his activities.

He doesn't hold your hand in public and at times seems disinterested.

He prefers dinners at home with you doing the preparations.

He calls you needy when you seek clarity about your future together.

He won't make it official after several months of dating.

He frequently cancels plans in favor of other activities.

He vanishes after one night of sex.

To protect yourself, remove the blinders and realize that some men want you forever and some for a limited time. Why waste time trying to convince a man who doesn't share your desire for a bond? As Maya Angelou said, "when someone tells you who they are believe them.". Stop excusing his behaviors that only hold you hostage. One self-proclaimed commitment-phobe said the idea of marriage felt like strangulation.

Chapter 21
The Psychopath

"Being with a psychopath doesn't just hurt your heart- it breaks your soul-it shatters it completely."

Unknown

On the hierarchy of manipulators, the psychopath reigns supreme. Savvy psychologist, Ellen Hendrickson reports that "psychopaths comprise 0.6% to 4 % of the population and exists in all cultures." All psychopaths aren't murderers although the one you're with can kill your dream of a pleasurable connection.

Psychopathy is a spectrum disorder which means it includes various traits. A true psychopath has most of the characteristics on a psychopathy checklist. Only a mental health professional using a proven list like Robert Hare's can accurately diagnose psychopathy.

The psychopath is a narcissist and like the narcissist he wears the letter,'I.' His hopes and dreams are all that matter. If you analyzed a psychopaths' goals, you'd see an overarching plan to take advantage of others physically, emotionally, mentally and financially without a shred of remorse. He is an extraordinary con-man who has perfected the art of seduction and can clothe himself in normalcy. If he mouths, I love you it's probably a lie since he is incapable of love.

A primary strategy is to mirror his victim. Her interests become his interest; he imitates her gestures, speech patterns and attitudes. He laughs when she laughs and finishes her sentences. He presents the illusion of perfect harmony. Remember he has fine-tuned his observation skills and reflects what she likes, responds to and wants.

He is a social chameleon because he can alter his personality to achieve his desired aim.

He relishes playing games for his excitement and entertainment. Before dumping her one victim said her psychopath lover admitted," I've been playing you the whole year." Her devastation meant nothing because psychopaths don't care if someone suffers as long as it isn't him. Remember, the person who cares the least controls the relationship.

Undergirding his self-confidence is arrogance and a sense of entitlement. His many stories cast him as the star in his drama. He portrays himself as a superior being who isn't required to follow rules. His quick and cocky responses take you down a notch to an inferior position. He uses sarcasm or rages when you challenge his authority.

Why is the psychopath labeled a puppet master? It is because he pulls behavioral strings to make the victim jump and become upset while toying with her emotions. According to Rhonda Freeman, neurophysiologist," puppets are expected to defend, agree with or sacrifice their reputation to protect" the psychopath. Freeman says, "it is often their preference to have numerous puppets."

Another tool in his arsenal is the psychopath's uncanny ability to figure you out speedily. He is adept at gleaning information about you from non-verbal cues like facial expression, eye gaze, gestures, hairstyles, and posture. One psychopaths' target said," he studied me with unnerving intensity."

You are the perfect dupe for a psychopath if you are love-starved, need emotional support or validation; possess weak self-confidence; socially submissive; desperate for a relationship; experiencing unbearable loneliness; new to an area and without close associates or family; recently lost a loved one because of death, divorce or breakup; have undefined personal boundaries; a risk-taker who craves an exciting partner; a sensitive empath who thrives on rescuing men or you're exceptionally trusting, loyal and supportive. One woman said her downfall was trusting him too soon. Insight dictates that you make an intimate earn your trust first. Remember the adage' trust but verify.' Keep in mind that "callous use of the lonely is a trademark of the psychopath," according to Robert Hare. Re-read the healthy ways to abolish loneliness mentioned in previous sections of this book.

Ladies, get to know yourself. Identify your weak spots and triggers. Self-awareness is a safeguard to protect you from the wiles of a predator. A woman's strength and weakness are to give her heart along with her body. It improves connection with a potential partner but is easily exploited by the devious.

Be suspicious when he doesn't have money for dates or concocts a story to justify moving in with you. He could be seeking someone who will pay the bills and provide uncommitted sex and free accommodations.

The psychopathic partner has a defective conscience untamed by moral behavior. He doesn't care who gets hurt as long as he is exempt. Don't expect him to understand your emotions because he lacks empathy. Given time his captivating charm will seem artificial. You'll notice his frequent lies and when challenged he'll change his account to fit the revision. Calling him out about the deceit is useless and will exasperate you. He has numerous excuses and will attempt to make you appear off-balanced. One psychopath said, "everyone lies, what's the harm?" One woman said her date told her an unbelievable lie she overlooked because she liked him. After he scammed her, she thought of the myth. Another person ignored her initial uneasiness because she wanted to accept the guy.

It is crucial to trust your gut reactions. In my twenties, I lived in Los Angeles, California. One morning while walking to a nearby store, the hair on my arms stood up. I looked to my left and two blocks away a man was looking in my direction. I felt an icy chill. I rapidly went back home and kept looking back to ensure he wasn't following me. I may have dodged a bullet. If you feel uncomfortable around a man, don't deny or rationalize the feeling -it may be your protection.

Should you expect fidelity from a psychopath? NO. According to psychopath expert, Robert Hare, the psychopath is promiscuous. Clinical psychologist, Seth Meyers says, "the psychopath engages in promiscuous sexual behavior or has many short-term marital relationships. Meyers states, "psychopaths don't engage in promiscuous sex because they love sex so much; It's more about boosting their ego when they feel rejected, obtaining power or defending against the boredom psychopaths often feel." Other experts have said the psychopath continuously searches for new victims. A contributor to LoveFraud.com says "psychopaths are very promiscuous and use women as tools to satisfy their desires."

Experts agree it is easier for you to enter the relationship than to leave. Once the psychopath has you in his trap of power, he wants to control your every thought and behavior. He may create a trauma bond and exploit you with verbal barbs, physical, emotional abuse or fear of abandonment. When you follow his script, he appreciates you, if you don't, he depreciates you. If you feel unworthy, you'll justify his behavior until he discards you. If you leave before his appointed time, he will love bomb you again to tempt you to return. Your best defense is not to become involved with this toxic person.

Resist this information at your peril; this is your opportunity to recognize truth and dispel the errors. Your desire for a man can cause you to blind yourself to reality. Then you'll be the pawn of this evil man who may shatter your heart, bury your dignity and steal your property. "He took my car and possessions" commented one woman." I had trouble finding him because he used a fake ID."

These signals can also protect you if you heed them.

Red Flags:

Significant people in your life don't like him.

He says you overanalyze everything or implies you're crazy when you question his actions.

He pushes your buttons and labels you overly sensitive when you react.

He makes several hurtful comments like "you're getting too old to compete with prettier, younger women" and then says you misunderstood him.

He demands to be the focus of your attention.

He is only concerned about his problems and challenges.

He doesn't walk his talk.

He wants to control how you spend your money.

You feel controlled or pressured.

He asks you to teach him how to love.

He begs you not to give up on him.

You start to feel depressed every time you talk to him.

He admits he beat-up a former partner.

He belittles your friends and family and isolates you from them.

He distorts truth with repeated lies.

He is very self-centered, arrogant and a braggart.

His initial flattery is excessive to make you feel like his perfect woman and then he changes to a criticism monster.

He seems too good to be true or initially makes you feel terrific before he switches to his authentic self.

He doesn't respect your boundaries.

He never apologizes for inappropriateness.

He breaks promises without remorse.

He blame shifts-attributing fault to others for his wrongdoings.

He exploits others for personal gain.

After your commitment he changes from charismatic and electrifying to cruel and uncaring.

He is cold-blooded towards suffering.

He craves power and control over others.

He is easily bored and needs external stimulation.

He only makes negative comments about previous business colleagues and friends.

He discloses confidential information early in the relationship. His motive may be to gain trust or to impress. If he repeats the same stories it may be to determine your gullibility.

If he asks multiple questions, he may be seeking information to use against you later; determine your vulnerabilities or identify the stressors from which to offer salvation.

He asks for special favors early and often.

He takes you on fantastic dates but has different reasons you must pay the bill.

His cold and empty eyes frighten you.

He makes odd comments like I'm 'psycho' or I can't help being enticed by women and then claims it was a joke. It may be to gauge your reaction or keep you off balance.

He disappears for several days without notice.

You can't shake the nagging feeling something is wrong with him.

Chapter 22
The Misogynist

"Vacillates between love and hate for women."

Are you surprised to know that men exist who will sell you a face ticket of love and respect while nursing an internal disdain for you? It's easier to detect the blatant haters because they don't hide their emotions. But the misogynist has a facade of sexiness, affability and charm designed to deceive and entrap you. Once he has you hooked his real emotions surface. These may include anger, disgust at your inadequacies, and jealousy about your achievements. His desire to manage every piece of your relationship rears its ugly head. His control arsenal includes cruel verbal abuse, yelling, humiliation, insults, non-stop criticism, blame and intimidation. He maintains his power position by taking charge of the finances and the frequency and type of sexual involvement. If he cheats, he says it's your fault for not satisfying his desire. Every part of your life with him has to be done his way. He pokes holes in your self-esteem until your self-confidence crumbles. He's like a seesaw up one minute down the next. You don't know what will cause an undesirable reaction- so you walk timidly.

According to expert Susan Forward, *Men Who Hate Women and The Women Who Love Them,* "a misogynist needs to control women." This need may originate from dysfunctional parenting and is used to control the man's fears and anxieties.

Misogyny is not listed as a mental disorder in the Diagnostic and Statistical Manual of Mental Disorders (DSM-5) because it is considered more of a belief system.

Some Christian women believe that the answer to avoiding a misogynist is to marry a Christian. I thought that too until I read *Christian Men Who Hate Women* by Margaret J. Rinck. She says these men use the same tools of intimidation, - verbal abuse, gaslighting, blame-shifting and rewriting history to control their partner. But the Christian misogynist attempts to legitimize his treatment with teachings from the bible. He tells his wife she isn't submissive or honoring her husband if she isn't obedient to his demands. Or he may claim that the husband has headship (complete) authority in the home; he leads, she follows. Another common ploy is to tell his wife that she must be subject to his demands to please the Lord. If the wife offers an opinion contrary to the husband's the husband may say the wife doesn't have authority over a man. He may frequently remind her that she is a weaker vessel and he is powerful and must be in charge. Finally, this husband tells his wife God created her for the man's sake, to be his helper.

If you want short-cut answers to the Christian misogynist's misinterpretation of the biblical teachings read *Is Christianity or the Bible misogynistic,* Matt Slick. To further protect yourself get a study bible, bible commentary and ask the Holy Spirit for wisdom and learn the proper biblical interpretation. You can decide truth for yourself.

Similar to the other toxic partners your best defense is recognizing the signs.

What does he think about powerful women?

What role does he believe a woman should have in personal and professional relationships?

Does he frequently criticize you and other women?

Who does he say should control the finances in a personal partnership?

Does he ridicule your ideas? (As a teenager, I dated a guy who chanted 'pretty girls have no brains, heads as clear as windowpanes.' I kicked him to the curb.)

He badmouths your female friend, colleagues or your sisters.

He is jealous and possessive. He wants complete control of your activities.

When angered he is verbally abusive.

He belittles you, everything you do is wrong according to Mr. fault-finder.

He reminds you of your childhood wounds to confirm your inadequacy.

Your intuition tells you he doesn't care about you as a person.

He wants to redesign you to be his ideal woman.

He blames you or women for everything that goes wrong in his life.

Final Word

I chose to focus on self-leadership after I trained as a coach. Leaders influence the thoughts and actions of other people. However, the first and most important person you impact is yourself. You can't avoid your self-review. Think about how your words or thoughts encourage or discourage you. Other people's disparaging comments may wound but you don't have to be around them. You can't escape from the constant stinking thinking if it lives in your head.

Isn't it time to realize the way you think about yourself is responsible for unsuitable men connecting with you? Have you selected men based on fear and low self-worth? Were you looking for a partner to heal the injuries created by thirst for a father? Or someone to patch the broken pieces of your life? Are you desperate to experience love? If you're like me, you desire the exhilaration of the initial stage of romance. Do you long for a family, to feel special or to eject the cavernous loneliness?

Have you heard the saying the way to wholeness is through brokenness? Doesn't that seem like an oxymoron? How can being broken create wholeness? Becoming broken or crushed can motivate you to seek relief from the pain. You may then become humble enough to eliminate self- deceit and self-reliance. Can you own what Wisdom Hunter says, "that it has been your leadership, your decisions, your strength and your self-sufficiency that has landed you in your current state?" As you consider the results of your choices you may decide that you can't manage life on your own. As some of the other women have come to terms with, you may realize that God is your only hope. When you accept the Biblical God as your father, Jesus Christ as your Savior and repent of your sins you receive the wisdom of the Holy Spirit who will guide you into all truth. When you become whole you won't be tempted to interact with a broken man.

Throughout this writing I've discussed reasons not to choose a partner or red flag awareness tips. Now, I summarize my advice for achieving a healthy partnership.

Develop a spiritual foundation as a reliable guide. Mine is Jesus Christ and I follow His law that says, "Love the Lord your God with all your heart, with all your soul, and with all your mind, and your neighbor as yourself." When you follow this Jesus principle, you can learn to love unselfishly. It is challenging to consider another person as more important than yourself but it is doable with God's help. Attached with that law is the Golden Rule that tells you to do to others what you want done to you. Some people prefer the Platinum Rule," Do unto others as they would have you do unto them."

Learn to accept and value yourself. Make peace with your worthiness for affection and a significant other. If you can't adore yourself, despite your flaws, you'll have difficulty when you discover your beloveds' imperfections. Remember, we're all under construction; the healthy person strives for self-improvement as part of a stable foundation of positive character.

Fine-tune your discernment skills. Observe and embrace the qualities that make a reliable mate. My essential character components are honesty, integrity, emotional intelligence, kind-heartedness, trustworthiness, flexibility, sense of humor and maturity. Financial stability is crucial. What are yours? Steve Harvey said "only become involved with a grown-up man." I learned from a past relationship the importance of a mate who supports your dreams. Forget the delusion you can be with someone you love but don't like. The, 'I don't like you but I love you' philosophy is a shaky myth. Your ideal person has made peace with any trauma from his past. Everyone has baggage but it shouldn't contain trash that will stink-up your interaction. If your character needs upgrading improve it before you seek your ideal mate.

Learn your love language, discover what makes you feel adored. Sharpen your understanding of what your partner means by love. Are your ideas similar? Internalizing your beliefs about what will make you content is an excellent way to maintain high standards and to only open the door to a person who will honor you.

Lust, a strong sexual desire, has blinded many an eye. As Lena Aburdene Derhally says," magnetic chemistry is great but don't excuse bad behavior because of it." You can't spend your life in bed; shouldn't a long-term partner possess other valuable attributes?

A friend told me she couldn't be herself with a man she valued. Do you hide your real self because you don't feel accepted by your lover? If you sense judgment or condemnation by your significant one, how can you relax in his presence?

A man who loves you will not deliberately hurt you. Unintentional wounds may occur but he will acknowledge, apologize, and not repeat the action. According to leadership expert John Maxwell, "a man is what he repeatedly does."

Thank you for reading this book. I hope the time you invested helps develop a healthier you and brings you the relationship of your dreams. I wish you peace and health. Feel free to contact me with your thoughts.

Your candid review of this book on Amazon would be a tremendous help. Please mention what you valued and what could be improved. Your comments would reveal if the information helped you grow and would assist me in improving my writing skills.

Cheryl Burton

References

Daddy Issues definition. Dictionary.com. Online dictionary.
http://www.dictionary.com.

Huang, C. (2019). 6 Types of Father-Daughter Relationships; The
Ruined Father (Video File) Psych2.net. Retrieved from
https://www.youtube.com.

Watts, P. (N.D) How the Addicted Brain Hijacks the Mind [Blog
Post] Retrieved from https://www.mentalhelp.net/blogs/how-the-
addicted-brain-hijacks-the-mind/

Brown, C. (2016). Daddy Issues: *How the Gospel Heals Wounds
Caused by Absent, Abusive and Aloof Fathers*. Retrieved from
www.Amazon.com/Kindle ed. /Humble Beast Records, Portland,
Oregon.

Dr. Prem Web Magazine (N.D.) Fatherless Daughter Syndrome:
Psychological effects of absent father on a girl. Retrieved from
https://drprem.com/globalhealthcare/fatherless-daughter-
syndrome-psychological-effects-of-absent-father-on-a-girl

Lancer, D. (2018) Recovery from codependency. Retrieved from
https://psychcentral.com/lib/recovery-from-codependency/.

Pikiewicz, K. (2013) "Codependent" no more? [Blog post] Retrieved
from https://www.psychologytoday.com/us/blog/meaningful-
you/201307/codependent-no-more.

Rosenberg, R. (2016) Breaking free to self-love from risk comes
freedom, codependency, resilience, courage. (Video file) Self-
love recovery.com. Retrieved from
https://www.youtube.com/watch?v=YmOv1maITbg

Mayo Clinic (2017) Stuttering, Retrieved from https://www.mayoclinic.org/diseases-conditions/stuttering/symptoms-causes/syc-20353572

Gilbert, Larry (N.D.) The Mercy-Shower. Retrieved from https://churchgrowth.org/do-you-have-the-spiritual-gift-of-mercy-showing/

Kirsch, J. (2017) The Science of Stepdads. Health Science Magazine. Retrieved from https://www.fatherly.com/health-science/science-how-to-be-good-stepfather-stepdads/

Deal, R. (2002) Stepparenting: It takes two. Focus on the family. Retrieved from https://www.focusonthefamily.com/parenting/stepparenting-it-takes-two/

Carter, L. (2019) A people-pleasers guide of do's and don'ts. Retrieved from https://www.youtube.com/watch?v=94tFX7S6iAA

How should I understand God as Abba Father? (N.D.) Retrieved from https://www.compellingtruth.org/Abba-Father.html

Nielson, L. (2014) How Dads Affect Their Daughters into Adulthood [Blog] Retrieved from https://ifstudies.org/blog/how-dads-affect-their-daughters-into-adulthood

Stanley, C. (2019) A Father's Influence In Touch Magazine. Retrieved from https://www.intouch.org/read/magazine/daily-devotions/a-fathers-influence

Muehlenberg, B. (2014) Dads4Kids, Daughters and Dads Fact Sheet. Retrieved from http://www.fatherhood.org.au/resources/DADS-AND-DAUGHTERS.pdf

Rannigan, R. (2013) Are you a distant dad? The Good Man Project. Retrieved from https://goodmenproject.com/featured-content/are-you-a-distant-dad-lbkr/

The Fatherless Generation (ND) [Blog] Retrieved from https://thefatherlessgeneration.wordpress.com/statistics/

American Heart Association News (2018) Why It's So Hard to Quit Smoking. Retrieved from https://www.heart.org/en/news/2018/10/17/why-its-so-hard-to-quit-smoking

Veland, C. *Stop Giving It Away* Codependency questions. Retrieved from advice column https://stopgivingitaway.com/

American Psychological Association (2020) Sexual Abuse. Retrieved from https://www.apa.org/topics/sexual-abuse/

Langberg, Diane (2003) *Counseling Survivors of Sexual Abuse,* symptoms and after-effects of sexual abuse*, pgs. 88-91* Xulon Press, printed in USA.

Mariottin, C. (2014) David and Tamar [Blog] Retrieved from https://claudemariottini.com/2014/03/24/the-rape-of-tamar/

Forcible rape in the United States since 1990. Retrieved from https://www.statista.com/statistics/191137/reported-forcible-rape-cases-in-the-usa-since-1990/

Gray, E. (2018) The Enduring Messy Power of Rage-Filled Women, Huffpost. Retrieved from https://www.huffpost.com/entry/angry-women-good-and-mad-rebecca-traister-rage-becomes-her-soraya-chemaly_n_5bb27285e4b027da00d65113

Mayo Clinic staff (2017) Antisocial personality disorder, Symptoms and Causes-Mayo Clinic [Blog] Retrieved from http://psycheblog.uk/2017/02/02/symptoms-and-causes-antisocial- personality-disorder-mayo-clinic/

Stout, M. (2015) *The Sociopath Next Door,* Harmony Books, USA.

Healing. Journey (N.D.) Understanding How Sociopaths Think: Why It Is Good to Ask Why. Retrieved from https://www.psychopathfree.com/articles/understanding-how-sociopaths-think-why-it-is-good-to-ask-why.278/

Perine, K. (2017) 5 Things Psychopaths and Narcissist Will Do in Conversation [Blog] Retrieved from https://www.psychologytoday.com/us/blog/brainstorm/201712/5-things-psychopaths-and-narcissists-will-do-in-conversation

Blakeley, K. (2013) 10 Signs Your Man Is a Psychopath [Café Mom's Blog] Retrieved from https://thestir.cafemom.com/love/164716/10_ways_to_know_in

Birch, A. (2013) Psychopaths & Love Do you have traits that make you vulnerable to psychopathic manipulation? [Blog] Retrieved from http://psychopathsandlove.com/traits-of-the-psychopaths-victim/

Meyers, S. (2014) Sex and the Psychopath [Blog] Retrieved from https://www.psychologytoday.com/us/blog/insight-is-2020/201410/sex-and-the-psychopath

Wise, J. (2010) How Psychopaths Choose Their Victims [Blog] Retrieved from http://jeffwise.net/2010/10/17/how-psychopaths-choose-their-victims/

Path victims (2016) Please Help Me I Am in Love with a Psychopath. Retrieved from http://psychopathvictims.com/victim-story/please-help-me-i-am-in-love-with-a-psychopath

Anderson, D. (2018) Why psychopaths do what they do. [Blog] Retrieved from https://lovefraud.com/the-answer-why-psychopaths-do-what-they-do/

Psychopathy (N.D.) Retrieved from https://www.psychologytoday.com/us/basics/psychopathy

Freeman, R. (2015) 6 Obstacles to a Relationship with a Psychopath [Blog] Retrieved from https://www.psychologytoday.com/us/blog/neurosagacity/201506/6obstacles-relationship-psychopath

Hendricksen, E. (2015) How to Identify a Psychopath or Sociopath, Scientific American, Retrieved from https://www.scientificamerican.com/article/how-to-identify-a-psychopath-or- sociopath/.

Tartakovsky, M. (2018) Surprising Myths and Facts About Antisocial Personality Disorder [Blog] Retrieved from https://psychcentral.com/blog/surprising-myths-facts-about-antisocial-personality-disorder/

Psychology Today (N.D.) Antisocial Personality Disorder. Retrieved from https://www.psychologytoday.com/us/conditions/antisocial-personality-disorder

Durvaula, R., Glossary of Narcissistic Relationships, YouTube videos, Retrieved from https://www.youtube.com/watch?v=4AkSWIquoaQ&list=PLVYfFCk_RTn5E2LXQm_HqsJNBfMJwxUvs&index=2

Neal, R., Why Won't Men Commit, (2002) Retrieved from https://www.cbsnews.com/news/why-wont-men-commit/

Cheryl Burton

Beachum, L. (2016) Prisons Around the World are Reservoirs of
Infectious Diseases. Retrieved from
https://www.washingtonpost.com/news/to-your-
health/wp/2016/07/20/prisons-around-the-world-are-reservoirs-
of-infectious-disease/

Black Demographics, (2018) Black Male Demographics in USA.,
Retrieved https://blackdemographics.com/

Beattie, M. (1990) Codependents Guide to The Twelve Steps, Simon
and Schuster, New York

DeMoss, N. (2001) Lies Women Believe and the Truth that Sets
Them Free, Moody Publishers, Chicago, Ill.

Hollander, D. (1995) 101 Lies Men Tell Women and Why Women
Believe Them, List of 101 Lies,

Harper Collins Publishers, United States of America

NAACP Criminal Justice Fact Sheet (N.D.) Retrieved from
https://www.naacp.org/criminal-justice-fact-sheet/

McGee, R. (1993) Father Hunger, Servant Publications, Ann Arbor,
Michigan

Hare, Robert (1980) Psychopathy Checklist-Revised (PCL-R)
Retrieved from https://psychology-tools.com/test/pcl-22

Bible Hub (N.D.) Luke 10:27- Jesus law: Retrieved from
https://biblehub.com/luke/10-27.htm

Firestone, T. (N.D.) Seven Qualities of an Ideal Partner, [Blog]
Retrieved from https://www.psychalive.org/seven-qualities-of-
an-ideal-partner/

148

Derhally, L. (2016) 10 Tips for choosing the Right Partner [Blog] Retrieved from https://www.huffpost.com/entry/choosing-right-partner_b_7688382

Baby Daddy, Urban Dictionary. Retrieved from https://www.urbandictionary.com/define.php?term=baby%20daddy

Wisdom Hunters, Benefits of Brokenness. Retrieved from, https://www.wisdomhunters.com/benefits-of-brokenness/

Branson, B. (N.D.)11 telltale signs you're in a misogynistic relationship, Retrieved from https://www.focusonthefamily.ca/content/11-telltale-signs-youre-in-a-misogynistic-relationship

Ivanovic, N. (N.D.) Misogynist Men: 18 Ways to Instantly Spot a Women Hater. Retrieved from https://www.lovepanky.com/women/understanding-men/misogynist-men-signs

Slick, M. (N.D.) Is Christianity or the Bible misogynistic? (Blog) Retrieved from https://carm.org/is-christainity-or-the-bible-misogynistic

Women's health.gov. (N.D.) Effects of Domestic Violence on Children, Retrieved from, https://www.womenshealth.gov/relationships-and-safety/domestic-violence/effects-domestic-violence-children

Child Sexual Abuse (N.D.) Retrieved from https://www.mosac.net/page/164

American Psychological Association (A.P.A.) (N.D) Sexual Abuse Retrieved from https://www.apa.org/topics/sexual-abuse/

National Institute of Drug Abuse (2020), Adolescent Brain Development, Retrieved from https://www.drugabuse.gov/news-events/news-releases/2020/04/landmark-study-adolescent-brain-development-renews-additional-seven-years

RAINN (N.D) Perpetrators of Sexual Violence Statistics. Retrieved from https://www.rainn.org/statistics/perpetrators-sexual-violence

MacArthur, J. *The MACARTHUR Study Bible, New King James Version,* 2 Samuel 13, pgs. 444-448

Illinois Coalition Against Sexual Assault, (ICASA) [N.D.] Acquaintance Rape. Retrieved from http://icasa.org/uploads/documents/Stats-and-Facts/aqr-fact-sheet-2012.pdf

Cocchimigillo, S. (2020) Traits of a High Functioning Sociopath. Retrieved from https://www.betterhelp.com/advice/sociopathy/traits-of-a-high-functioning-sociopath/

Hayes, S. (2015) In Love with a Sociopath, Retrieved from https://hubpages.com/relationships/Sociopath

Chelin, A. (1981) The 50's Family Life and Today (Opinion), New York Times, Retrieved from https://www.nytimes.com/1981/11/18/opinion/the-50-s-family-and-today-s.html

Colbert, D. (1971) *Deadly Emotions,* Introduction, pg. xi, Thomas Nelson Publishers, Nashville, USA

Other Books by Cheryl Burton

This book explores twenty aspects of learning to influence yourself and improve your personal and professional connections. Learn the reasons self-leadership is vital. Delve into teachings that range from mastering motivation, improving self-confidence, dealing with difficult people to crafting your life legacy. Get it today from Amazon.com as a paperback or on Kindle.

https://www.amazon.com/s?k=Mastering+the+Art+of+Self-Leadership

Complimentary 'E' book

Discover the unintentional actions that hinder your success. Available as a complimentary E-book on Amazon.com https://www.amazon.com/s?k=Stop+Limiting+Your+Success&i=digital-text&ref or a free download at https://www.cheryleads.com.

Free Quiz

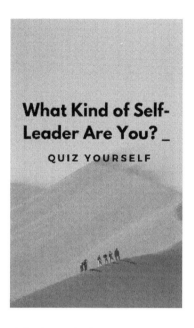

Test your self-leadership knowledge. Use the list of twenty questions and determine if you are a phenomenal, average or weak self-influencer. I have included an explanation of each category. Available as a gift at https://www.cheryleads.com/

While at my website https://www.cheryleads.com/ check out my Blog section for more knowledge on enhancing your self-leadership. My Facebook page at https://www.facebook.com/maximizeselfcb has helpful articles for your growth. You can also contact me for personal coaching on Facebook, at https://www.facebook.com/maximizeselfcb if you desire an accountability partner to assist in your development.

About Cheryl

Cheryl Burton is a John Maxwell certified coach specializing in self-leadership. Cheryl is also certified as a Christian counselor through the American Association of Christian Counseling, (AACC). Before retirement she served as a registered respiratory therapist for forty years on medical teams that managed cardiopulmonary diseases. Cheryl taught respiratory therapy at Forest Park community college, St. Louis, MO. and Malcolm X Community College, Chicago, Illinois, where she was also the respiratory therapy program director. Cheryl earned the Advanced Communication Gold and Advanced Communication Silver certificates through Toastmasters International. She is currently honing her skills as an author to help the reader improve their personal growth, self-awareness and self-leadership.

Her coaching business is Leading in Success, LLC. Follow Cheryl on Facebook at https://www.facebook.com/maximizeselfcb

Printed in Great Britain
by Amazon

57187828R00099